Così fan tutte, An Opera of Mimetic Revelation

STUDIES IN VIOLENCE, MIMESIS, AND CULTURE

SERIES EDITOR
William A. Johnsen

The Studies in Violence, Mimesis, and Culture Series examines issues related to the nexus of violence and religion in the genesis and maintenance of culture. It furthers the agenda of the Colloquium on Violence and Religion, an international association that draws inspiration from René Girard's mimetic hypothesis on the relationship between violence and religion, elaborated in a stunning series of books he has written over the last forty years. Readers interested in this area of research can also look to the association's journal, *Contagion: Journal of Violence, Mimesis, and Culture.*

Così fan tutte, An Opera of Mimetic Revelation

Isabel Díaz-Morlán

Michigan State University Press · *East Lansing*

Michigan State University Press
East Lansing, Michigan 48823-5245

LIBRARY OF CONGRESS CATALOGING-IN-PUBLICATION DATA
Names: Díaz Morlán, Isabel, 1967– author.
Title: Così fan tutte, an opera of mimetic revelation / Isabel Díaz-Morlán.
Description: [First.] | East Lansing : Michigan State University Press, 2025.
Series: Studies in violence, mimesis, and culture
Includes bibliographical references and index.
Identifiers: LCCN 2024057106 | ISBN 9781611865448 (paperback)
ISBN 9781609177904 | ISBN 9781628955538
Subjects: LCSH: Mozart, Wolfgang Amadeus, 1756–1791. Così fan tutte. |
Opera—Psychological aspects. | Libretto. | Mimesis in music. |
Mimesis in literature. | Music and literature.
Classification: LCC ML410.M9 D529 2025 | DDC 782.1—dc23/eng/20250110
LC record available at https://lccn.loc.gov/2024057106

David Drummond, Salamander Design, www.salamanderhill.com.
Illustration from 19th century, iStock.

Visit Michigan State University Press at *msupress.org*

¿Qué humor puede ser más raro
que el que, falto de consejo,
él mismo empaña el espejo,
y siente que no esté claro?

What kind of mind could be stranger
than he who ill-advised
steams up the mirror
and then moans that it is not clear?

—SOR JUANA INÉS DE LA CRUZ (*SÁTIRA FILOSÓFICA*, 1689)

Contents

Illustrations

Tables

Musical Examples

Preface

For many readers of René Girard, their first encounter with his work is something of a revelation as they discover how well his mimetic theory elucidates so many aspects of human behavior. In particular, Girard demonstrated how certain works of literature are capable of revealing these behaviors, exposing their characters' true motivations and what was driving them to act in the way they did. The purpose of this book is to ascertain whether these manifestations of human mimetic behavior can also be found in opera, in the same way that Girard discovered them in the classics of literature. To this end, I propose to study the opera *Così fan tutte*, the last of the three created by Wolfgang Amadeus Mozart and Lorenzo Da Ponte.

Così fan tutte was first performed in Vienna on 26 January 1790. Although the score has always been admired for its musical beauty, its libretto received widespread criticism almost immediately after the premiere. As a result, neither the public nor the critics fully understood the artistic coherence of this work until well into the twentieth century. Since then, however, the negative response to Da Ponte's libretto has been under review and several fruitful advances have been made in research into the origins of the story it tells. In this way, leading scholars of this opera have uncovered the amalgam of literary sources on which the librettist drew and analyzed the recurring elements that crop up in so many of them, as well as the numerous links between them. Yet, many differences of opinion remain concerning the true significance of the text, especially because of the power of the music, which tends to mask the meaning attached to the words and actions.

Various Mozart scholars cite *El curioso impertinente*, the famous *novela* inserted in the first part of Miguel de Cervantes's *Don Quijote de la Mancha*, as a fundamental source of the libretto. As might be expected, the literary studies of *El curioso impertinente* do not mention its links to the Mozart opera, although some explore its relationship with René Girard's mimetic theory. A case in point is *"Monda y desnuda," la humilde historia de Don Quijote* by Cesáreo Bandera,[1] which includes a study of *El curioso impertinente* from the point of view of mimetic desire. This was based on Girard's own analysis of *El curioso impertinente* in his book *Mensonge romantique et vérité romanesque*.[2] *El curioso impertinente* has been identified as one of the sources of *Così* by various musicologists and as a vehicle of mimetic revelation by Girard and Bandera. It therefore struck me that perhaps *Così fan tutte* could also be analyzed from a Girardian perspective as a potential source of mimetic revelation. This initial intuition led to further investigation, and as I went deeper and deeper into the musical and literary analysis of the opera, I began uncovering a whole array of literary sources, many of which had connections with mimetic theory. Clear links also appeared between mimetic theory and both the music and libretto of *Così fan tutte*. Finally, overwhelmed by so much data and worried that in the end it might be impossible to prove that the laws of desire, as explained by Girard, were revealed in this opera, I decided that the only way to find out would be to put it all down in writing. The result is this book.

Rather than using Girard's theory as a framework within which to gain a better understanding of the opera, my initial idea was to use the opera to gain a clearer picture of Girard's hypothesis, as he himself did in his analysis of many of the classics of literature.[3] The object therefore is not to study the opera in a bid to prove that it confirms many of the ideas of mimetic theory, but rather to understand what it reveals about the truth of human mimetic behavior.[4] In other words, although Da Ponte and Mozart were clearly unaware of this theory, it is equally clear that they had an acute understanding of human behavior and that perhaps they were trying to reflect that knowledge in *Così fan tutte*, just as other authors have done in literature. If novels, tragedies, and comedies can reveal mimetic behavior, perhaps operas could do so too, especially an opera like *Così*, whose libretto owes much to sources that also reveal mimetic desire. As we shall see, the fact that Girard never analyzed any particular opera in depth, although he did mention them on occasion in his published interviews, should in no way be considered an obstacle to my attempt to apply his ideas in the analysis proposed here.

In order to "put it all down in writing," I thought it best to begin by explaining, in chapter 1, how the opera came into being and the reasons for its somewhat tardy acceptance by public and critics. Chapter 2 seeks to familiarize readers with the storyline and structure of the opera, without which it would be difficult to follow the subsequent analysis. Chapter 3 deals with the literary sources of the libretto, starting with a general description of all the sources found before comparing them with the libretto for *Così fan tutte*. By this point, the thematic motifs discussed in the analysis that follows should be clear. However, before embarking on the analysis, I have decided to insert chapter 4, which lays out the basic principles of René Girard's thought on mimetic desire as revealed in literary works. This chapter also proposes how this theory might be applied to operatic works. The book concludes with chapter 5, which analyses the opera from the perspective of mimetic theory, on the basis of the motifs uncovered in the comparison of the literary sources, and taking into account the interaction between the music, the text and the dramatic action. The book is rounded off with a brief epilogue that, on the basis of my analysis, seeks to provide an answer to the initial question regarding the possible links between *Così fan tutte* and mimetic theory that gave rise to this research.

In the bibliography at the end of the book, I have decided to include the editions in Spanish that I have read, in the hope that this information may be of interest to Spanish-speaking readers, especially with regard to the classics and the works by René Girard. In the latter, I have also added the title and date of the original editions.

Throughout the book, the reader will find many literal quotations from various authors. I am aware that too many quotations can interrupt the narrative flow, sometimes annoyingly. However, in this case I feel they are justified. The aim is not to appear erudite or to cement my ideas with weighty references, but to highlight the astonishing coincidence between many of the ideas put forward by the scholars of this opera and Girard's theory, even though none of these scholars actually cites him by name.

I am most grateful to the following people who read the manuscript and offered me so many excellent suggestions as to how to improve it: Ricardo Ortiz de Urbina, Rosa Morlán, Pablo Díaz-Morlán, Patricio Goyalde, Maite Aseginolaza. I would also like to thank Nigel Walkington for his thoughtful translation from Spanish to English, and Ben Heschmeyer for the accurate transcription of the musical examples. Finally, I would like to emphasize how grateful I am to William Johnsen for his support and his belief in the value of this book.

CHAPTER 1

Creation and Reception of *Così fan tutte*

In the ten years between the serious operas *Idomeneo* (1781) and *La clemenza di Tito* (1791), W. A. Mozart wrote four comic operas for the theatergoers of Vienna: a singspiel entitled *Die Entführung aus dem Serail* (1782) and three *opere buffe* with librettos by Lorenzo Da Ponte, *Le nozze di Figaro* (1786), *Don Giovanni* (Prague 1787, Vienna 1788), and *Così fan tutte* (1790). This succession of comic operas was not accidental and is usually understood as an effort on the part of Mozart to please Emperor Joseph II, first with an operetta in German and later with several operas in the Italian comic style, which the emperor preferred to more serious works. *Così fan tutte* was to be the last of these productions, as its premiere coincided with the emperor's death.

As Bruce A. Brown and John A. Rice revealed in 1996, Lorenzo Da Ponte first offered his libretto for *Così* to Antonio Salieri in October 1788. However, after writing a few numbers, Salieri abandoned the project.[1] A year later, in November 1789, Da Ponte offered the libretto to Mozart, who immediately set to work. Mozart replaced the original title, *La scuola degli amanti* (The school of lovers), which probably sounded to him like a "neutral lesson in moral philosophy,"[2] with *Così fan tutte* (So do they all), a much more direct and provocative title, which would also enable him to design subtle musical games within the opera.[3] This sequence of events completely overturns the theory that it was Mozart, worried about his wife's probable infidelity, who came up with the idea for the libretto. On similar lines, some authors have insisted on trawling through real events in the hectic love lives of Da Ponte and his contemporaries in order to justify his decision to make the fidelity test a key theme in the libretto for Mozart's new opera. In my opinion, to write a good libretto, or indeed any good story, it is not necessary for the author to have actually experienced the events they describe. In this case, it would have been sufficient for Da Ponte to have been an attentive observer of human behavior and interpret it through his deep-seated knowledge of the classics.[4] Another suggestion is that the story was inspired by a recent event in Vienna that the emperor thought would make a good subject for a libretto. This theory does not stand up either: first, because in 1789 Joseph II was embroiled in the war against the Turks and became very ill. He was therefore in no fit state to commission new operas and even less to propose frivolous themes for new librettos[5]; second, the literary sources for the libretto (some very ancient and all traditional) are so abundant that there is no doubt that the plot was crafted around them.

Mozart completed the opera less than three months later, and by the end of the year he had arranged a private performance at home, to which the composer Joseph Haydn and Mozart's friend Michael von Puchberg were invited.[6] A dress rehearsal was held five days before the public premiere,[7] which took place on 26 January 1790 at the Burgtheater, Vienna's most famous theater. It was attended by roughly a thousand people, and Mozart himself wielded the conductor's baton. There were five more performances until February 11, which were more successful at the "box office" than any other opera that season. It seems that Mozart was quite well remunerated, earning twice what he received for *Figaro*, although he expected even more.[8] If, in addition, we take into account that excerpts from the opera were published shortly after the premiere,[9] all the signs were that the opera would be successful and that Mozart would reap the rewards for his efforts.

However, Emperor Joseph II, who was already ill when the opera premiered, soon took a turn for the worse and died on February 20, after just ten performances. The theater was closed for two months, and by the time it reopened, Mozart's new opera was no longer new. It had a few summer performances, which brought in very limited earnings, and Viennese audiences did not see it again until 1794, by which time the composer himself had died. In the meantime, there were premieres in Prague (1791), Dresden (1791, with a shortened version), and Leipzig (1791, 1792, and 1793), which were received with ovations,[10] more for Mozart's music than for the libretto.[11]

In fact, few people seemed to appreciate the story that was told in this opera even at the time, as it was deemed offensive towards women. Criticism was frequent throughout the nineteenth century, and it was not until the mid-twentieth century that a cautious rehabilitation began, although most scholars, with the exception of Alfred Einstein and Edward Dent,[12] continued to view the libretto as inferior to the music. The lasting impression of all this skepticism about the libretto is that *Così* has long been misunderstood. Critics have tended to focus on its moments of great beauty while dismissing the opera as a whole as lacking the necessary coherence to be considered a great work of art.[13]

However, an article published by Ernst. H. Gombrich in 1954 proved something of a watershed, in that he was the first scholar to reveal that *Così*'s libretto drew on classical sources. Since then, several studies have appeared showing how closely the text feeds on traditional stories or themes,[14] and this insight has restored much of the missing coherence to the plot. In other words, we now know that Da Ponte constructed his libretto using elements drawn from the classics, which he combined with a clear, deliberate intention that we will later go on to unravel.

Another line of research has also appeared in which *Così* is assessed within the theatrical and intellectual currents of the era in which it was created. The findings of various researchers demonstrate that the ideas that *Così* is putting forward regarding the impossibility of perfect fidelity or idealized romantic love should not be seen as incoherent, nor can they be put down to an arbitrary whim or poor workmanship on the part of the writer, and instead should be viewed as exploring a theme that was perfectly embedded in European enlightened thought. According to Charles Rosen's pioneering study of 1971,[15] *Così* is a perfect example of what he calls the "comedy of experimental psychology" typical of the eighteenth century. *Così* should be understood as a process or demonstration of a law of human nature. This means the significance does not lie so much in the problem and how it is resolved, but in the process—in the steps taken by the main characters as they, perhaps unknowingly, comply with the laws of human behavior when they are subjected to an experiment whose outcome is preordained. In other words, according to Rosen, the characters are victims of an inexorable law, from the eighteenth-century point of view of human nature. The problem is that he does not explain what this point of view, this law of human nature, consists of. Will men and women be unfaithful if incited to do so? He doesn't say. In any case, this view changed in the nineteenth century with the shift towards romantic idealism. This may be one of the reasons why the opera was not accepted, or not understood, until much later on.

In addition to Rosen, other researchers have also tried to interpret *Così* within the framework of the literary and philosophical currents in vogue at the time. Like Rosen, Isabelle Moindrot[16] described this opera as a product of the experimental psychology of the eighteenth century, a demonstration of the universal laws governing human behavior; Jean-Michel Brèque[17] and Brown[18] classified the work within the tradition of *scuole* or demonstration comedies, a subgenre of opera buffa that used theater as a vehicle for passing on the sentimental education typical of the time; Mary Hunter[19] argued that *Così* contained all the conventional themes of opera buffa, among them the female fidelity test. In addition, Stefan Kunze and Andrew Steptoe[20] affirmed that love's true mechanisms are revealed in *Così*, while for Charles Ford[21] the opera is a defense of the materialist theories that emerged during the Enlightenment.[22] In short, all these interpretations have a common theme running through them, namely that the opera provides a truthful demonstration of a specific form of human behavior. This conclusion, if true, would allow us not only to refute the prejudiced opinions as to the incoherence of the plot and its supposed contempt for women, but also to explain why public appreciation of the libretto was so short-lived. It would also encourage us to take a more direct approach to the study of this opera, to take it "seriously," as it were.

Let us accept, then, that this opera does indeed reveal authentic human love behavior. If so, what exact form does this behavior take, or what does this universal law consist of? If we observe the work "as is," without trying to interpret it in any way, the answer lies in the title, which roughly translates as "So do they all" or "All women do that." The key word here is "that" rather than "all." In this case, "that" refers to the alleged fickleness of women who would readily change the object of their affection as soon as the object they possess moves away and a new one appears on the scene. This is exactly what happens to Dorabella and Fiordiligi, the main female characters. And this is exactly what Girard discovers in those literary works that, in his eyes, reveal the truth, or what he calls the "novelistic truth," as opposed to the "romantic lie."[23] Let us suppose, with Girard, that love, or rather desire, is always dependent, induced, or mimetic, and that this was revealed or made visible in *Così fan tutte*. If we accept that the Romantic literature of the early nineteenth century transformed the vision of that love or desire by emphasizing its independent, spontaneous, absolute nature, it is clear that the Romantics could not possibly understand the intention of an opera like *Così*, which sought to tell the truth and reveal the authentic human condition, which had little to do with that portrayed in Romantic fiction.

CHAPTER 2

Summary of the Plot and Structural Relationships

As a theatrical work, *Così fan tutte* is very austere. It has only six singers and five simple sets (coffeehouse, chamber, hall, garden, and little garden), and there are no special effects except for the scene in which the main characters are "healed" by a magnet, which does not require many props either. According to Christoph Wolff,[1] this scenic austerity was due to the fact that Austria was at war at the time of the premiere; in fact, even within the plot, war is the natural backdrop against which the story unfolds.

The action begins in a *bottega di caffè* (a coffeehouse) in the city of Naples, where two young, inseparable friends, Ferrando and Guglielmo, meet an older man, Don Alfonso, who casts doubt on the fidelity of their fiancées, the sisters Dorabella and Fiordiligi. The disagreement between the two friends and the old man ends with them accepting a wager: They agree to submit the women to a fidelity test, which the men are convinced they will pass with flying colors. The whole scene works musically as an *introduzione*, developed by means of three tercets in the tonic chord keys (G-E-C), which alternate with two recitatives.

In the following scene (2), which takes place in the two sisters' garden, we are transported to a much more feminine atmosphere. The two women sing a duetto, in which they compete with each other, exalting the qualities of their beloveds. Don Alfonso enters and begins to set the whole deceitful farce in motion: He announces that the two young men have been called away to war and must leave forthwith. From scene 3 to scene 7, we watch the lovers play out a long farewell, in which, amidst the expression of the most painful affections, apparently sincere in the girls and feigned in the boys, they are hounded by the sound of a military march summoning them away.[2]

Inside the house and once alone, Dorabella and Fiordiligi tell their maid, Despina, what has happened. Dorabella expresses her despair in an exaggerated way, in an aria that mocks the serious style of the infernal arias of opera seria. Despina then tries to cheer them up by reminding them there are many more fish in the sea ("You lose those two, but all the rest are left"). In this way, she tries to incite their desire for others while at the same time casting aspersions on the capacity of their betrotheds to remain true. The sisters are shocked at such suggestions and finally the three women leave the room (scenes 8 and 9). Then Don Alfonso enters (scene 10). He calls Despina and convinces her to let two exotic young foreigners enter the house. The two foreigners are none other than Ferrando and Guglielmo disguised as "Albanians," who will try to seduce the women as part of the wager. Despina accepts, unaware of their knavish plan.

In scene 11, the two "foreigners" enter the house. Don Alfonso tries to smooth their entry by pretending they are old friends of his. We witness the first attempts to seduce Dorabella and Fiordiligi, and although the men's advances and flattery are rejected, it is clear that Dorabella's curiosity has already been piqued, while Fiordiligi declares that she is firm "come scoglio" (like a rock), in an aria sung in a tone of exaggerated rejection. Once the men are alone, in scene 12, they laugh at Don Alfonso, gleefully believing that their sweethearts have passed the test. But Don Alfonso refuses to accept defeat and returns to conspire with Despina, who proposes a new ruse (scene 13).

This is followed by the finale of act 1 (scenes 14 to 16), which is set in a small garden, where the two sisters sing a duetto to mourn their absent lovers. Suddenly the two "Albanians" take the stage, followed by Don Alfonso. In the midst of great wailing and screaming, the two men pretend to take poison and start writhing around as if on the point of death. The girls' compassion and their fear for the young men's lives break down the remaining obstacles preventing them from approaching the men and touching them. Meanwhile

Despina and Don Alfonso exit, allegedly to look for a doctor, leaving the sisters and young men alone. Don Alfonso returns with a "doctor," who is in fact Despina in disguise. She then sets to work with a "mesmeric stone," or healing magnet,[3] with which she miraculously cures the "dying Albanians." Once revived, the two men again shower the girls with compliments and flattery, and their resistance begins to crumble, although in the end they decide to reject the men firmly. However, the sisters' highly histrionic protests hint that they will be yielding to the men before too long.

The first three scenes of act 2 take place in a room of the house in which both sisters and Despina are present. Contrary to our expectations, given the resolute spirit with which they ended the first act, the sisters now appear hesitant, willing to let Despina lead them on. In the end they surrender, in a duetto in which they decide "whose is whose" ("Which of these two Narcissi do you fancy for yourself?"). In this way, each girl chooses the other's fiancé without realizing. However, for the moment, their decision to yield to their new beaus is nothing more than an intimate confession between the sisters, a private game in which their only intention is to have a little fun. The audience, however, knows it will not be long before the two men discover that neither of the sisters will be passing the test.

We are now in the garden, the ideal place to enact the final stage of the courtship. In scenes 4 and 5, from a male duetto we move to a quartet involving all four protagonists, from which the duetto between Dorabella and Guglielmo, the first mixed duet of the opera, breaks off. In this brief symmetrical succession of numbers, we are privy to the fall of Dorabella, who throughout the opera has been the more fragile and less thoughtful of the two sisters. Fiordiligi, however, is a much harder nut to crack. Her fall takes seven scenes (6 to 12), in which there are five arias, four *accompagnati* recitatives, and a change of scenery. Throughout all these numbers, Ferrando has to fight against the pain he feels over Dorabella's betrayal, against his own fury, and even against Fiordiligi's sudden attack of remorse. Fiordiligi, for her part, has to cope with the frivolity of her sister, who after succumbing to her new love is now urging Fiordiligi to do likewise, openly espousing Despina's opinions. Fiordiligi also has to weigh up and resolve the doubts that are growing inside her. She expresses them in a heartfelt aria-rondo, "Per pietà" (Out of pity), and in a recitative in which she declares that she is determined to go to war in male disguise to seek out her fiancé, Guglielmo. But all her efforts come to nought when Ferrando suddenly appears and the recitative is transformed into a skillfully seductive duet, in which she finally gives in to his entreaties.

Although brief, the next two scenes (13 and 14) prior to the grand finale provide the climax of the plot. The three men are left alone on the stage. Guglielmo's disappointment is exacerbated by Ferrando's vengeful sneer, but both are silenced by Don Alfonso, who victoriously proclaims, "Così fan tutte," which is repeated with resignation by the other two.

The finale necessarily involves the whole truth being revealed, when the two sisters and Despina, who was unaware of the wager or that the men were in disguise, discover that they have been tricked. To this end, Don Alfonso has come up with another ingenious ploy, the immediate celebration of the new couples' weddings. Everything is arranged for their betrothals in a large, well-lit hall. The introductory music, in the affirmative C major of the Overture, gives no clues as to possible obstacles. Despina, a blind collaborator until the end, appears disguised as a notary. Once the marriage contracts are signed and just when the two women think that their happiness is complete, we hear the same military march in D major that sounded in the first act, when the two soldiers left for the war. The news of their unexpected return provokes a chain reaction and a whole array of mixed feelings (confusion, regret, anger). The music too is with changes of meter and modulations, including some minor modes. When the men's deceit is finally revealed and all that remains is the truth, the original couples, though justifiably upset with each other, are finally reconciled and come together, in the triumphant key of C major, to intone a serene reflection: Let us be content with the good things we have, and let reason be our guide; given that weakness is an inescapable, inherent part of being human, it is better not to put it to the test.

As a summary of the main storyline to which readers can refer, Table 1 sets out the most important moments in the plot, together with the scenes and the places in which they occur. The main theme of *Così* is not, as it might first appear, a wager on the fickleness of womankind, but rather on the inevitable, uncontrollable nature of human behavior: People, when encouraged to do so, will always desire the things they do not possess and will readily betray everything they have to obtain them. This hypothesis is announced at the beginning, in the title, as a law of human behavior. It is then put to the test and proven by demonstration: Events unfold before our eyes and ears that will prove the hypothesis is true. Action, words, and music are arranged to suit this demonstrative purpose. However, this truth is only demonstrated for one sex, the female, and this has "crucial repercussions" in the structure,[4] in that only two falls from grace need to be shown rather than four. This allowed Mozart and Da Ponte to articulate the second act around just two key moments.

Of course, the structural requirements of the opera buffa as a genre must also be considered. These include an even number of acts, the construction

TABLE 1. Most important moments in *Così fan tutte*

<table>
<tr><th colspan="3">ACT 1</th></tr>
<tr><th>SCENE</th><th>PLACE</th><th>ACTION</th></tr>
<tr><td>Overture</td><td></td><td></td></tr>
<tr><td>1</td><td>coffeehouse</td><td>the two friends FD & GL
+
doubts sown by DA
+
wager</td></tr>
<tr><td>2</td><td rowspan="2">garden</td><td>the two sisters DR & FL</td></tr>
<tr><td>3–7</td><td>terrible news
+
lying farewell</td></tr>
<tr><td>8–10</td><td rowspan="2">room</td><td>incitement to desire by DP
+
conspiracy 1: DA-DP</td></tr>
<tr><td>11–13</td><td>the two strangers: seductions through flattery
+
test fails (except for small weakening DR)
+
conspiracy 2: DA-DP</td></tr>
<tr><td>14–16 Finale</td><td>little garden</td><td>seduction by appealing to their compassion (poisoning and healing by mesmerism)
+
signs that DA was right (crumbling resistance of DR & FL, and excessive female rage)</td></tr>
</table>

TABLE 1 (*continued*)

<table>
<tr><th colspan="3">ACT 2</th></tr>
<tr><th>SCENE</th><th>PLACE</th><th>ACTION</th></tr>
<tr><td>1–3</td><td>room</td><td>the two sisters privately admit their desires</td></tr>
<tr><td>4–5</td><td rowspan="2">garden</td><td>DR’s fall (duet)</td></tr>
<tr><td>6–9</td><td rowspan="2">FL’s fall (duet)</td></tr>
<tr><td>10–12</td><td rowspan="2">room</td></tr>
<tr><td>13–14</td><td>truth revealed to the two men: “Così fan tutte”
+
conspiracy 3: DA-DP</td></tr>
<tr><td>15–17 Finale</td><td rowspan="2">hall</td><td>fictitious weddings by false notary</td></tr>
<tr><td>17–18</td><td>military march: return of FD & GL
+
truth revealed to the two sisters
+
reconciliation of original couples and acceptance of the truth</td></tr>
</table>

Note: The names of the characters have been abbreviated as follows: Ferrando (FD), Guglielmo (GL), Don Alfonso (DA), Dorabella (DR), Fiordiligi (FL) and Despina (DP).

of the scenes according to the principles of variety and alternation of styles (i.e., recitative/melodic, long/short), the equal distribution of arias among the characters, the mandatory two finales, and the established conventions within the various musical styles (overture, recitatives, arias, duets, ensembles, choruses). Table 2[5] shows the place of the duets between the numbers of the opera. This allows us to observe the specific pairings of characters and actions over the entire course of the opera, so enabling us to better understand how the law of human behavior is demonstrated over time. This was done according to a carefully designed, premeditated strategy.

If we look at the tables, we can see that the first two duets in each act follow a very similar pattern, in that in both cases the first duet is sung by women and second by the men. The other two duets appear in act 2, in which the results of the experiment, or the surrender of the two sisters, must be revealed. This surrender in fact takes place at two different times in two

TABLE 2. Distribution of duets between the numbers of the opera

ACT 1	1	2	3	4	5	6	7	8	9	10	11	12	13	14	15	16	17	18

ACT 2	19	20	21	22	23	24	25	26	27	28	29	30	31

Note: The numbers shaded in gray and black denote female (4 and 20) and male duets (7 and 21) respectively, and the diagonal grid denotes mixed duets involving Dorabella (23) and Fiordiligi (29).

duets, cleverly spaced quite far apart by Mozart and Da Ponte, with two main purposes: first, to highlight that each woman has her own, quite different character, and that one is much better at controlling her desires than the other; and second, to ensure that the audience's interest in the action does not wane, and in fact continues in gradual crescendo, after the duetto by Dorabella and Guglielmo, and throughout the five arias (numbers 24 to 28) that come between it and her sister's duetto with Ferrando.

Another aspect that can help us understand the particular structure of this opera is the symmetrical design of the pairs of characters and of the relationships between them. If we look exclusively at the relationships that occur between the four (or perhaps six, when Ferrando and Guglielmo disguise themselves) young people, how many couples are formed throughout the opera with just these characters? If we accept that at the end we have the same couples as at the beginning, as many as seven different pairs can be identified (see Table 3). In the first act we have five pairs, three of which are doubles (the original male friends, the sisters, and the fictitious male friends), and two are mixed (the original couple, Ferrando-Dorabella and Guglielmo-Fiordiligi). In the second act, two new mixed pairs are formed by crossing the original pairs (Ferrando-Fiordiligi and Guglielmo-Dorabella). The doubles are broken or separated, their members having distanced themselves from each other in terms of their actions and emotions, albeit only momentarily. Finally, in the denouement, the four original pairs, doubles and mixed, are reunited. In fact, these final pairs could also be considered new pairs, because at the end of the drama they appear to us in a new light: wiser than at the beginning of the play and, we suspect, less in thrall to the romantic ideal, because they now know that true, unchanging love or desire is impossible.

TABLE 3. Double and mixed pairs in *Così fan tutte*'s plot

<table>
<tr><th>DOUBLE PAIRS</th><th colspan="2">MIXED PAIRS</th><th></th><th></th></tr>
<tr><td rowspan="2">FD & GL
DR & FL</td><td>FD & DR</td><td>GL & FL</td><td rowspan="2">Initial Situation</td><td rowspan="4">ACT 1</td></tr>
<tr><td colspan="2">Initial pairs: apparently authentic</td></tr>
<tr><td rowspan="2">The two
“Albanians”</td><td>FD & FL
Sensitive &
suffering
Parte serie</td><td>GL & DR
Frivolous & parodic
Parti buffi</td><td rowspan="2">Test</td></tr>
<tr><td colspan="2">Intermediate pairs: truly authentic</td></tr>
<tr><td rowspan="2">FD & GL
DR & FL</td><td>FD & DR</td><td>GL & FL</td><td rowspan="2">Final Situation</td><td rowspan="2">ACT 2</td></tr>
<tr><td colspan="2">Final pairs: truly inauthentic</td></tr>
</table>

Plot designs based on “wife swapping” were typical of eighteenth-century comedies such as those by the French playwright and novelist Pierre de Marivaux. The debt owed by Da Ponte’s libretto to the “romantic comedies of Marivaux” was explored by Daniel Heartz, who highlighted that “they often deploy two young couples who are manipulated by an older, more philosophical friend into discovering their true selves.”[6] For her part, Constanze Natošević remarked on the similarity of the themes explored in various Marivaux comedies to the plot of *Così*, adding also that in the years prior to the premiere of the opera, many plays and operas staged in Vienna were centered on a fidelity test and partner swapping.[7] The influence of Marivaux’s comedies was also analyzed by Steptoe in his study of the plot of *Così*. He argues that the libretto exploits “the variety of interaction made possible by the permutation of the lovers . . . typical of an eighteenth-century design that was perfected by Marivaux.”[8] Thus, the six characters responsible for moving the action and the storyline forward are grouped in pairs who act as doubles of each other and in pairs who can interact and, in the case of the lovers, interchange. This creates a structure of relationships, which Steptoe depicts in a diagram.[9] This diagram clearly expresses the symmetry of the different permutations of pairs of lovers and also the parallel, and to some extent symmetrical, behavior of Despina and Don Alfonso, who act as confidants and collaborators of the female pair and the male pair respectively. However, the diagram fails to capture the linearity of the plot, whose most important

TABLE 4. Similarities between the scenes and settings in acts 1 and 2

ACT 1		ACT 2	
SCENES	**SETTINGS**	**SETTINGS**	**SCENES**
1	interior *bottega* the two friends dominate the scene	interior *camera* the two sisters dominate the scene	1–3
2–7	exterior *giardino* the two sisters start with a duet	exterior *giardino* the two friends start with a duet	4–9
8–13	interior *camera*	interior *camera*	10–14
Finale 14–16	exterior *giardinetto*	spacious interior *sala*	Finale 15–18

event, the test, moves in just one direction, from the men to the women, thus preventing a symmetrical design. It perhaps also falls short when describing Despina and Don Alfonso as "confidants," in that, in my opinion, it does not reflect the real influence of Despina on the two sisters as an inciter of desire, nor that of Don Alfonso on the two friends as an inciter of doubt.

Other scholars besides Steptoe have highlighted the symmetry that dominates the structure of this opera. José Luis Téllez, for example, talks about the "duplication of symmetrically arranged events," so that "each situation in the first act has . . . an inverted duplication, in the second," and affirms that the music "complements and discusses, subtly and decisively, the iron symmetry of the literary structure."[10] However, he offers no examples to support these claims. In fact, my analysis suggests that this symmetrical structure is not as "iron-clad" as it may seem, although I have observed, when comparing the structure of the two acts, a very similar alternating pattern of scenarios and a similar musical and dramatic organization within the first scenes of each act. These similarities are set out in Table 4.

As we can see in the table, the alternation between interior and exterior spaces is almost the same in both acts. From an enclosed place, a public coffeehouse in the case of the men in act 1 and a private room in the case of the women in act 2, we move to the garden, only to return to the interior of the house. The two finales, however, have different settings. The first takes place in a small garden, while the second happens in a large room.

Mozart and Da Ponte make skillful use of typical scenarios for seduction such as a room inside the house and the garden of the house. In act 1 the girls hear the first blandishments of their false lovers in a room inside the house, although the most intense seduction episode, the poisoning, takes place in a small garden. In act 2 the seduction starts in the garden, where Dorabella quickly gives in, and then ends up moving indoors, where, after a much longer, more drawn-out process, Fiordiligi finally capitulates. In other words, in the first act the seducers pursue the women from the inside to the outside of the house, while in the second act they pursue them from the outside (with relative success) to the inside (with complete success). And what is interesting is that while Dorabella and Guglielmo shamelessly consummate their union in a public, almost improvised promenade, Fiordiligi and Ferrando need more intimacy, albeit for different reasons: Ferrando wishes to charm Fiordiligi while she is alone and defenseless, whereas Fiordiligi requires the protection of solitude to be able to repudiate everything she has been so loudly proclaiming up until then.

CHAPTER 3

The Literary Sources of the Libretto

In a brief article published in 1954, E. H. Gombrich stated that the libretto for *Così fan tutte* drew greatly on the myth of Cephalus and Procris, and in particular on the version recounted in Ovid's *Metamorphoses.*[1] Since then, various new discoveries have been made about the literary sources of *Così*, which offer us a much more complete picture of the amalgam of stories on which Da Ponte based the libretto.[2] I decided to gather together all the works, ancient and more recent, in which fundamental events (or parts thereof) in the libretto of *Così fan tutte* also appear, obtaining a lengthy list. All these different works are set out in Table 5, which includes the following information: the date of composition, publication, or premiere; the author, the title, and, where appropriate, the part of the work in which the story is found; and finally, the key element linking each work to the libretto of *Così fan tutte.*

This is a very extensive, heterogeneous list, which as a whole is perhaps not fit for purpose, in that it does not trace a direct genealogical line. A quick overview reveals some very influential classics, such as Ludovico Ariosto, Cervantes, and William Shakespeare, but it would be interesting, looking at the list chronologically, to analyze the fine details of the different stories, compare them, and finally try to identify and extract the various thematic

TABLE 5. Possible literary sources for the libretto

DATE	AUTHOR	WORK	LINK WITH *COSÌ*
1 B.C.	Hyginus	*Fables*, 189	Cephalus & Procris
1 B.C.–A.D. 1	Titus Livy	*The History of Rome*, 1.58–60	Collatinus, Tarquinius & Lucretia
A.D. 1	Ovid	*Fasti*, 2.725–834	Collatinus, Tarquinius & Lucretia
A.D. 1	Ovid	*Metamorphoses*, 7	Cephalus & Procris
A.D. 1–2	Pseudo-Apollodorus	*Mythological Library*, 3.15	Cephalus & Procris
1353	G. Boccaccio	*Decameron*, 2.9	Bernabò, Ambrogiuolo & Zinevra
1532	L. Ariosto	*Orlando furioso,* 1.18–19	the two friends Cloridano & Medoro
	L. Ariosto	*Orlando furioso,* 1.24	names of Fiordiligi (faithful), Doralice (inconstant) & Fiordespina (passionate)
	L. Ariosto	*Orlando furioso,* 2.27	comparison between female fidelity and the phoenix
	L. Ariosto	*Orlando furioso,* II 28	the two friends Astolfo & Iocondo
	L. Ariosto	*Orlando furioso,* 2.43	chained stories: the cup trial, the Knight of the Po, and Anselmo, Adonio & Argia
1605	M. de Cervantes	*El curioso impertinente,* in *Don Quijote*, 1.33–35	the two friends Anselmo & Lothario and Camila
1605	M. de Cervantes	*Don Quijote*, 1.24, 27–29, 36	double couples: Cardenio & Luscinda and Fernando & Dorotea
1610	W. Shakespeare	*Cymbeline*, comedy	the two friends Leonatus & Iachimo and Imogen

TABLE 5 (*continued*)

DATE	AUTHOR	WORK	LINK WITH *COSÌ*
1618	G. de Castro	*El curioso impertinente*, theater play	the two friends Anselmo & Lothario and Camila
1621 and 1635	Tirso de Molina	*La celosa de sí misma* and *El amor médico*, comedies	similarity of themes: two ladies married to two brothers, Don Alonso/ Don Alfonso, the maid Quiñones, the farewell scene, the rapid change of disguise, the comparison with the phoenix, the scene with the pedantic language doctor
1671	A. Behn	*The Amorous Prince or The Curious Husband*, comedy	plot based on Cervantes's *El curioso impertinente*
1694	J. Crowne	*The Married Beau or The Curious Impertinent*, comedy	plot based on Cervantes's *El curioso impertinente*
1710	Ph. Destouches	*Le curieux impertinent*, comedy	plot based on Cervantes's *El curioso impertinente*
1731	P. Metastasio	*Demetrio*, 2.iii, opera libretto	comparison between female fidelity and the phoenix.
1756	A. Palomba	*Il curioso del suo proprio danno*, opera by N. Piccinni	plot based on Cervantes's *El curioso impertinente*
1761	A. Palomba	*Il curioso imprudente*, opera by N. Piccinni and A. Sacchini	plot based on Cervantes's *El curioso impertinente*
1764	unknown	*Il curioso indiscreto*, opera by F. M. Gherardeschi	plot based on Cervantes's *El curioso impertinente*

TABLE 5 (*continued*)

DATE	AUTHOR	WORK	LINK WITH *COSÌ*
1771	C. Goldoni	*Le pescatrici*, opera by F. L. Gassmann	similarity of themes: the two friends, the two sisters, the wager, the disguise, the seduction by deception
1777	G. Bertati	*Il curioso indiscreto*, opera by P. Anfossi	plot based on Cervantes's *El curioso impertinente*
1778	C. Mazzolà	*La scuola de' gelosi*, opera by A. Salieri	two couples confronted by jealousy
1778	P. Marivaux	*Die Kinder der Natur*, singspiel by F. Aspelmayr (trad. of *La Dispute*, 1744)	double couples, female infidelity
1785	G. B. Casti	*La grotta di Trofonio*, opera by A. Salieri	similarity of themes: philosopher Trofonio/Don Alfonso, couple swapping.
1786	L. Da Ponte	*Il finto cieco* and *Una cosa rara*, operas by G. Gazzaniga and V. Martín y Soler	precedents of characters, texts and scenes
1787	L. Da Ponte	*L'arbore di Diana*, opera by V. Martín y Soler	precedents of characters, texts and scenes
1804 posthumous	G. B. Casti	*Il ritorno inaspetatto*, novella	husband's abandonment of wife because of war, and arousal of desire by a stranger

Sources: Created by the author with data taken from Livermore, "'Così fan tutte': A Well-Kept Secret"; Steptoe, "The Sources of 'Così fan tutte': A Reappraisal"; Heartz, "Mozart and Da Ponte"; Link, "*L'arbore di Diana*: A Model for Così fan tutte"; Brown, *W. A. Mozart Così fan tutte*; Goehring, *Three Modes*; Cochran, "Da Ponte, Mozart, Byron, Casti: A Question of Dimensions," and Scamuzzi, "Ovidio e Cervantes nella cultura di Da Ponte," "Tra Bradamante e Fiordiligi c'è Camila," *Il "curioso impertinente" fra Spagna e Italia*, and "Los dos amigos: Boccaccio, Cervantes, Guillén de Castro."

elements used in the plot of *Così fan tutte*. We should begin by examining each source separately. First of all, we have the works of classical antiquity, from the first century B.C. to the second century A.D., in which the myth of Cephalus and Procris (Hyginus, Ovid, Pseudo-Apollodorus) and the story of Collatinus, Tarquinius, and Lucretia (Titus Livy, Ovid) are narrated in different versions. Let's examine the details of these two stories.

The initial love between Cephalus and Procris is perfect. Problems begin when Cephalus strays too far from home; while out hunting, he is kidnapped by the goddess Aurora, who pressures him to be unfaithful with her. Cephalus refuses, and the goddess lets him leave but warns that he will regret returning to Procris. On his way home, Cephalus begins to doubt whether his wife has been faithful to him in his absence. There is actually no evidence of this, except for the goddess's warning, but Cephalus fuels his own doubts by marveling at his wife's youth and beauty. He decides to test her with gifts, to which end he disguises himself with the help of Aurora. Unlike the other versions, in the Hyginus rendering of the myth it is Aurora, feeling rejected by Cephalus, who skillfully makes him doubt Procris ("I do not want you to fail in your fidelity, unless she has failed first"—Hyginus 189, 3). To test her fidelity, the goddess changes Cephalus's appearance beyond recognition and supplies him with gifts, confident that if suitably flattered by a stranger, Procris will fall for him.

In all the versions of the tale, Cephalus decides to test Procris's fidelity, the only difference being that in Hyginus's account, the seeds of doubt are sown by someone else (the role played by Don Alfonso in *Così*), while in the other versions it is the husband himself who decides to act, without the need for external encouragement (as in Cervantes's *El curioso impertinente*). In any case, the result of the test is the same: Procris succumbs, and when the truth is revealed, she flees to the forest full of shame and indignation, to devote her life to the goddess Diana and turning her back on men forever, thus breaking up the couple. However, sometime later Procris returns and forgives Cephalus, and the two spend many happy years together. This part of the myth has strong parallels in Da Ponte's libretto, as in *Così fan tutte* there is incitement to doubt, disguise, a test, a fall, anger, and reconciliation. The tragic end suffered by the spouses in the myth is not, however, reflected in the opera: Procris gives Cephalus an "unerring" dart that never misses its target. One day out hunting, he hears a rustle in the bushes and hurls the dart, accidentally killing Procris.

The story of Collatinus, Tarquinius, and Lucretia as told by Livy consists of various episodes, of which the first two are of particular interest for my purposes. In a Roman camp far away from Rome itself, some princes and officers are having a party. The conversation turns towards the subject of their wives, and each man begins to extol the virtues of his beloved. Collatinus challenges them all by claiming that no woman is more faithful than his wife, Lucretia, and proposes that they should all return to Rome there and then to find out. They decide to pay their wives a surprise visit, during which they discover that all the women spend their time flitting from party to party, except for Lucretia, whom they find at home spinning thread. It seems that the story has come to a happy ending, at least for Collatinus and Lucretia, and the men all return to the camp. However, the foolish Collatinus has unintentionally planted the seeds of envy in the king's son, Sextus Tarquinius, who is filled with a desperate desire to possess Lucretia. A few days later, Tarquinius sets off again to visit Lucretia's house without Collatinus's knowledge. After unsuccessfully trying to seduce Lucretia, he violently forces himself upon her. As is well-known, Lucretia then summons her husband and various relatives, and confesses to them what has happened, directly accusing Tarquinius. She then takes her own life, stabbing herself with a dagger. This tale contains various themes: the two friends, the doubt about the wife's fidelity, the test (in this case the wife is tested twice, first by Collatinus and then by Tarquinius), and, finally, the desire to possess the other's prized possession.

The next source is Giovanni Boccaccio's *Decameron*, from the fourteenth century, one of whose stories tells the tale of Bernabò, Ambrogiuolo, and Zinevra.[3] It all begins in much the same way as the story of Collatinus, Tarquinius, and Lucretia. Various Italian merchants are at an inn in Paris. After dinner, they begin talking about their wives. They are all convinced that, in their absence, their wives are cheating on them. The merchants are then joined by Bernabò, who declares that his wife, Zinevra, is an exception to this rule. He extols the virtues of his lady with such passion that he arouses the mockery, and indeed the desire, of the young Ambrogiuolo, who declares that, in his experience, "the only chaste woman is she who has never been begged by anyone." Bernabò is angry and proposes to Ambrogiuolo that he should try to seduce Zinevra, betting that he will fail. The young man accepts the wager and leaves for Genoa to carry out the test. However, once there and after hearing reports of the lady's reputation for chastity, he decides not to approach her openly. With the help of one of Zinevra's female friends, he arranges to be carried into her bedroom at night hidden inside a chest. Once inside the room, he steals some personal objects and takes note of certain details of her sleeping body. Armed with this evidence, he returns to Paris, convinces the husband that his wife has been unfaithful, and wins the wager. Bernabò then commissions a servant to murder his wife. Nevertheless, Zinevra manages to convince the servant to let her flee, disguised as a man, and to tell his master that he has killed her. In return, she promises she will go far away and never return. However, after various adventures, the three protagonists meet again, and all is revealed. Ambrogiuolo is punished, and Bernabò and Zinevra are reconciled and reunited. In this story, we again find two friends, or at least two similar men, the exaltation of the desired object, the incitement to doubt, the reckless wager, and the test. There is also the deceived husband, because even though Ambrogiuolo does not even attempt to seduce Zinevra and bases his claims on fabricated "evidence," Bernabò does believe he has been betrayed. Finally, it is interesting to note that throughout the story, the reader is repeatedly assured that cheating on husbands is "what all women do," a phrase that is very reminiscent of Da Ponte's "*Così fan tutte*."

In the sixteenth century, Ariosto's *Orlando furioso* was undoubtedly a great repository of stories and themes for many later generations of writers. In fact, this epic poem contains at least five different stories that could have served as sources for Da Ponte: that of the two friends Cloridano and Medoro (18–19), the two friends Astolfo and Iocondo (28), and the chained stories of the cup test, the Knight of the Po, and Anselmo, Adonio, and Argia (43). Based on earlier work by Kurt Kramer, Brown cites these possible sources and also points out other possible links with Ariosto's poem.[4] On the one hand, *Orlando furioso* has characters called Fiordiligi (faithful), Doralice (inconstant), and Fiordespina (passionate), who appear in canto 24 and may well have served as inspiration for the female characters in *Così*. There is also a character called Isabella, whose name may have been combined with "Doralice" to produce "Dorabella." On the other hand, Ariosto evokes the image "come scoglio" in canto 44 (v. 61), which is exactly the same image evoked by Fiordiligi in her principal aria, along with some imprecations similar to those appearing in Dorabella's twin aria "Smanie implacabili." There are also other similarities in both imagery and form, especially of verse type associated with specific moments in the action. Finally, Ariosto (27) also makes the same comparison between women's fidelity and the phoenix (something that exists but no one has seen), as Don Alfonso does in the first scene of Mozart's opera.[5] Brown concludes that the libretto of *Così* is a kind of "Ariostan Capriccio" that combines borrowed elements with newly invented ones and successfully weaves them into a coherent whole.[6]

We should now look more closely at some of the details of the different stories. The only shared theme with the story of Cloridano and Medoro is that of the two friends or doubles. There is no fidelity test or anything of the sort, and instead it tells the tale of an unbreakable friendship between two men that ends tragically. For its part, the story of Astolfo and Iocondo offers us an example of double couples and explores the theme of female infidelity: As in the other stories, two men, the handsome King Astolfo and the equally good-looking Iocondo, are crestfallen when they discover that their wives have been unfaithful to them in their absence. They react by deciding to devote themselves to the unlimited seduction of women. After finding that not a single woman can resist their charms, they decide to return to their wives, who "are just the same as all the others of their sex." Indeed, the spirit of *Così* seems to be very present here in that, in the opera too, the protagonists also return to their original partners after realizing how inconstant all humans can be when desire rears its head.

Finally, the three stories from canto 43 share many common features with *Così*, such as the incitement to doubt women's fidelity, how unwise it is to put this to the test, the disguise, the disillusionment and reconciliation, and, in particular, the idea that all women are the same and that it is foolish to believe in them, even though they must be forgiven. All the stories in this canto spring from the hero Rinaldo's encounter, during his travels, with a knight from Mantua, traditionally known as the Knight of the Po. During a dinner at the knight's palace, the latter invites Rinaldo to drink from a magic cup which, he claims, will reveal the truth about his wife's fidelity. Rinaldo refuses to drink from the cup, saying that he prefers "not to know" what is "best not to know." This wise attitude prompts the knight to confess his own unfortunate story. Happily married, his happiness was interrupted by the sorceress Melissa, who had fallen in love with him and pursued him to no avail for some time. Feeling scorned, Melissa took revenge by sowing doubts in his mind about his wife's fidelity while, at the same time, offering him a way to be sure of her. In a similar way to Aurora in the myth of Cephalus and Procris, Melissa disguised the knight as one of his wife's former suitors to enable him to try to seduce her. Once he had managed to seduce her, the knight revealed who he was and how he had tricked her, at which the knight's wife turned on him in anger, announcing that she had decided to leave him and join her true love. After hearing this exemplary story, Rinaldo continues on his way. He takes a boat along the river, and during the journey, he strikes up a conversation with the oarsman about the recent events in his life. In a bid to reassure Rinaldo that he was right not to put his wife to the test, the oarsman tells him the story of Judge Anselmo. Married to the beautiful and chaste Argia, he nevertheless feels an imperious need to confirm that she is being true to him, in this case by consulting an astrologer. Meanwhile, with the help of some magical creatures, Argia's former lover Adonio succeeds in seducing her, so confirming Anselmo's fears. He then orders someone to murder his wife, but as in the Boccaccio story, this terrible deed is never actually carried out because the wife manages to escape in time. At that moment, the boatman exclaims: "How much more preferable would that doubt have seemed to him, if he had only reflected on the pain that the truth would cause him!" He then concludes his story by explaining that after several momentous events in his life, Anselmo himself was caught committing adultery, and this caused the spouses to come to their senses and forgive each other.

El ingenioso hidalgo Don Quijote de la Mancha by Miguel de Cervantes, one of the most famous works in Spanish literature, was published at the beginning of the seventeenth century, in the baroque era. *Don Quijote* contains a "story within the story" (1.33–35) entitled *El curioso impertinente* (The impertinently curious man). In this short story, which is little more than a drop in the great ocean that is *Don Quijote*, Cervantes brings a new, original human dimension to some of the elements identified in the earlier classical sources. It proved so successful that it became internationally known in its own right.

Let's take a closer look at the plot: The two friends here are Anselmo (who has the same name as the character in Ariosto's canto 28) and Lothario, while the woman in dispute is Camila. Anselmo and Camila are happily married, and are a model of fidelity and mutual love (as are Cephalus and Procris, Collatinus and Lucretia, Bernabò and Zinevra, Astolfo/Iocondo and their respective wives, the Knight of the Po and his wife, and the judge Anselmo and Argia). In this story, there is no need for a third party to sow the seeds of doubt. Anselmo fuels his own unease, creating a rival to provide the proof of his wife's fidelity that he claims he wants. In fact, what he longs for is to desire once again, as "what he feels is that the object of his desire, the beautiful, sensitive, intelligent, noble Camila no longer attracts him the way she used to."[7] The only way to rekindle this desire is to create an obstacle between him and his wife, in the person of his inseparable friend Lothario, whom he asks to try to seduce Camila. Once his initial scruples have been overcome, Lothario reluctantly gets down to the job. In the process, he begins to fall in love with Camila, and this in turn inflames Camila's desire for Lothario. When Anselmo discovers what is going on, tragedy ensues: Camila abandons him, taking refuge in a monastery (as Procris did in the service of Diana); Lothario escapes and ends up dying in a battle; and Anselmo dies alone, ill and chastened by his inappropriate, impertinent curiosity.

Rival doubles, the imitation of desire, foolish doubt, and a fidelity test come together in this influential story, which within a year of its publication had been adapted for the theater by the Spanish playwright Guillén de Castro.[8] From that moment until the end of the eighteenth century, Cervantes's story of the husband with a foolish wish would travel the world in multiple translations, adaptations, and versions, including several operas. According to Iole Scamuzzi,[9] in the almost two hundred years between the publication of Cervantes's short novel and the premiere of *Così*, at least eight versions of the story had been produced in play or opera format, as shown in Table 5. With the exception of the two English comedies, which date from the eighteenth century, I would agree with Scamuzzi that "*El curioso* fascinated the academies of the early seventeenth century, then fell silent for a century before flourishing again in the theater under the influence of the Spaniard Guillén de Castro."[10]

Don Quijote contains various other stories told to Don Quijote and Sancho Panza during their travels, which have also been identified as sources for some of the themes explored in *Così*. For example, as a possible source for the scene in which the lovers fake their suicide as a way of persuading the girls to succumb, Kramer proposed a story told to Don Quijote within the context of Camacho's wedding (1.20).[11] In this story, a young man called Basilio stages his suicide to be able to marry Quiteria, the woman he loves, *in articulo mortis* (at the moment of death). Kramer also states that faked suicide was a recurring theme in sixteenth-century literature and later reappeared in the librettos of seventeenth- and eighteenth-century operas. This means Da Ponte could have borrowed this idea from another source.[12] Another story from *Don Quijote* centers on double pairings and seductions (1.24, 27–29, 36). In this story, Cardenio tells of his love for Luscinda and about how he was betrayed by his friend Fernando, who seduced Luscinda while he was away. Fernando's betrayal is twofold, in that by seducing Luscinda he also is cheating on Dorotea, his fiancée. Finally, the two original couples are reconciled and reunited. This story was taken up by Shakespeare in a long-lost play called *Cardenio* (1613).[13] Much more interesting, however, is his comedy *Cymbeline* (1610), probably inspired by Boccaccio, which recounts the story of Posthumus Leonatus, Iachimo, and Imogen. In this story, Imogen and Leonatus are secretly married against the wishes of King Cymbeline, who, when he learns of this, banishes Leonatus. Now far away from his wife, a nagging doubt wells up within him, accompanied by an unconscious need to rekindle his desire for her. He makes a wager with his friend Iachimo that he will not be able to seduce Imogen. The rest of the story is very similar to that of the *Decameron*: Faced with the impossibility of seducing the lady, Iachimo is carried into her chamber hidden in a chest. He takes a careful look at her sleeping body and then returns to his friend with false proof of his wife's infidelity. Believing himself betrayed, the husband orders a servant to kill Imogen, but she escapes and hides, disguised as a man. After multiple adventures, involving a war with Rome, all is finally revealed, Iachimo is punished, and the spouses are happily reunited, with the blessing of Cymbeline.

Still within the seventeenth century, I could also mention various comedies by the Spanish playwright Tirso de Molina in which Ann Livermore found traces of *Così fan tutte*.[14] In her study, among other elements of the plot she cites a scene from *El amor médico* (Medical love) (1635), in which a fake pedantic doctor uses Latinisms. This could be seen as a precedent for Despina's mesmerism scene in *Così*. Likewise, in *La celosa de sí misma* (Jealous of herself) (1621) we find double couples, an emotional lovers' farewell, quick changes of disguise, an old matchmaker (named Don Alonso) who arranges the weddings, hasty agreements to carry them out before a notary, and even the ubiquitous metaphor of the phoenix. These are undoubtedly common themes, which can also be found in other baroque plays, for example in those by Molière, a better-known playwright whose work is studied all over the world.[15] However, these references to Tirso de Molina show that these were recurring themes in Spanish literary tradition, which had an unquestionable influence on later European theater.

Throughout the eighteenth century, and closer to home for Mozart and Da Ponte, various possible source plays were performed that the authors of *Così fan tutte* may have heard about or perhaps even seen.[16] Of particular note is Carlo Goldoni's comedy *Le pescatrici* (The fisherwomen), which was used several times as an opera libretto, for example by Florian Leopold Gassmann in Vienna in 1771. The similarities with the plot of *Così* are undeniable.[17] The play opens with two friends, each in love with the other's sister, another fine example of double couples. To test the fidelity of their beloveds, the friends disguise themselves and begin courting the women. Infidelity soon ensues, the friends reveal the deception, and, finally, a wise old man intervenes and brings the two couples back together, admonishing the men for their imprudence and advising all of them to forget the past.

More recently, another possible source for the libretto has been proposed, namely the satirical novels written by the Italian cleric Giovanni Battista Casti in the eighteenth century. According to Peter Cochran, "The satires of Casti—especially the *Novelle Galanti*, . . . in their comedy and their prismatic depiction of men and women, have much in common with *Don Giovanni*, *Le nozze di Figaro*, and *Così fan tutte*."[18] He identifies one novel in particular: *Il ritorno inaspettato*, about a youth who is overwhelmed by an unconscious desire for the woman next door, who has been left alone by her husband who went off to fight in a war. In my opinion, the most interesting aspect of Cochran's study is the conclusion he reaches regarding the meaning of the opera when examined from the perspective of satire. He claims that the central idea of the libretto is that love, "supposedly the great motive power of life, is a transferable emotion, the object of which is irrelevant."[19] Although Cochran does not refer to Girard, some of the concepts he uses, such as "transferable emotion" and "irrelevant object," are surprisingly similar to those used by Girard, so much so that I will return to Cochran when I analyze *Così* from the perspective of Girard's mimetic theory.

As mentioned earlier, another probable source within eighteenth-century literature was the comedies of Marivaux, some of which had been translated and performed in Mozart's Vienna. Like *Così*, these plays are genuine demonstrations of the laws governing human behavior, revealed through psychological experiments.[20] The audience enjoys watching the characters respond to a sequence of new situations filled with deceit and trickery, and laughs as their reactions expose their vanity, hypocrisy, and envy. Ultimately, however, this culminates in a happy ending, as required by the genre. It is interesting to note that in one of his first studies of literary works, Girard studied the hypocrisy of some of Marivaux's characters.[21] His findings will be analyzed later in this book.

Finally, I should highlight several operas, almost all performed in Vienna in the 1770s and 1780s, with librettos containing themes from earlier works that also feature in *Così fan tutte*, such as the two friends, the doubts about female fidelity, the wager, the test, the seduction by deceit, the couples torn apart by jealousy, or the judgmental philosopher character, among others.[22] These operas include *Il curioso indiscreto* by Pasquale Anfossi (Rome 1777, Vienna 1783, with a libretto by Giovanni Bertati), directly based on Cervantes's novel through Guillén de Castro; *La scuola de' gelosi* (Venice 1778, with a libretto by Caterino Mazzolà) and *La grotta di Trofonio* (Vienna 1785, with a libretto by Casti), both by Salieri; and finally, some librettos by Da Ponte himself, such as those composed for Vincente Martín y Soler (*Una cosa rara*, Vienna 1786; *L'arbore di Diana*, Vienna 1787) and for Giuseppe Gazzaniga (*Il finto cieco*, Vienna 1786). Some of these operas belong to the genre known as "pastoral drama," whose influence on the storyline for *Così fan tutte* has been suggested by various authors. In research into *L'arbore di Diana*, Dorothea Link found that both these Da Ponte librettos follow the conventions of pastoral drama (the love affairs, the magician, the horseplay) and try to answer the same question: "What is love?"[23] Edmund J. Goehring expressed a similar line of thought when he asserted that the "pastoral mode" had an undeniable influence on *Così fan tutte*, a claim that he set out to prove over the course of an entire chapter, in which he put forward a whole array of arguments, such as the analysis of Despina as Cupid.[24] In the end, however, he concluded that pastoral drama was not as important a source as Link made out and even asserted that, in the final scenes of *Così*, the pastoral vision is rejected as being too narrow "to offer a fully compelling vision of human nature."[25] For my part, I would add that the question "What is love?" is too wide-reaching and too universal to be evidence of the influence of the pastoral in *Così*. It is also possible that the nature of love might not be so important in the opera if we consider it solely as one of the ways in which mimetic human behavior manifests itself, as I will later go on to propose.

One obvious conclusion of this survey of the sources is that all these stories contain various elements that are repeated over and over again. We appear to be listening to the same story, which, in different ways but with the same basic intention, is leading towards an uncomfortable truth: namely, that absolute love is an illusion, since the true human condition is one of weakness, doubt, and fragility produced by a perpetual, innate dissatisfaction that pushes us to seek constant renewal of our desires. The purpose of these stories is to warn us about the dangerous drift in the inevitable human condition. However, although this purpose was undeniable in the sources, does this necessarily imply that the libretto of *Così fan tutte* was written with the same intention? To gain a clearer idea, I will continue with the comparative analysis and turn to the themes featured in the opera.

Comparative Analysis of Classical Sources

Of all these sources, which ones did Da Ponte actually draw on when he picked up his pen to begin writing the libretto for *Così*? It is impossible to know exactly. Da Ponte was a learned man who was familiar with the classics. It seems likely that he read Cervantes directly and of course Ariosto, of whom he was a great admirer.[26] These stories may also have reached him, as we have seen, through the filter of contemporary works, especially plays and operas, which he perhaps used as a basis for his libretto.[27]

As Brown and Rice argued, the presence of classical literary themes in the libretto of *Così* was not a question of chance.[28] Da Ponte was tailoring the libretto to the needs of Salieri, the composer for whom it was originally intended, rather than to those of Mozart. To this end, he drew on a diverse range of sources, in a sort of intertextuality that was perhaps intentional. Intertextuality, an important concept in literary criticism, contends that literary texts are never entirely original, and always refer to other texts, within a framework that spans centuries.[29] We therefore need to find out how this blend was created and what its ingredients were—in particular regarding the traditional sources, those prior to the eighteenth century. These sources offer greater consistency and less dispersion in the treatment of themes than later comedies and operas, and it is also plausible to imagine that Da Ponte knew and read these stories directly.

With this in mind, the next stage of my analysis will involve creating a list of the recurring themes in the classical sources that touch on doubts about fidelity and a fidelity test; identifying the sources; and analyzing the presence or absence of these themes in the sources and in the libretto for *Così fan tutte*. In this way, I hope to identify both the links between the main themes explored in *Così fan tutte* and the classical sources, and the possible existence of branches in the different versions of the story that would allow me to classify them into groups based on the particular themes selected by each one.

I compiled the list of themes, first by dividing the plot into five key moments mentioned in all the sources: (1) the initial situation, (2) the incitement to doubt, (3) the test, (4) the result of the test, and (5) the final situation. For each of these five key moments, I then looked at the possible variants in the different versions of the plot. All the stories begin with a pair of men. Sometimes the pair is formed by two friends or doubles, who will later become rivals, while in other cases the double is created by the husband as himself and in disguise. In *Così fan tutte*, these two situations are blended, as the two friends become rivals for each other, and they also become rivals for their alter egos when they change their identities through disguise. There is also a female double couple, which is quite unusual in classical sources, in that it only occurs in Ariosto (28) and in the Cervantes's story of Cardenio. The second key moment is the incitement to doubt. In all the sources, desire is aroused when someone—often an external agent, perhaps a magician or goddess, or a wise man with experience of life—begins to praise the desirable object. It could also be a friend and confidant, or a rival double. In some cases the doubts are raised by an internal agent, such as the husband himself. There may also be a facilitator, often a woman. The main characters in all these stories, either explicitly or implicitly, have doubts regarding their lover's fidelity, in that simply by agreeing to do the test, they are allowing that fidelity to be questioned. There may or may not be a wager, but there is always a test. This is the third key moment. The fundamental objective of the test is to successfully seduce the woman concerned and demonstrate her infidelity, for which various different strategies are employed: flattery and gifts that pique her desire and break down her resistance, disguises that hide

TABLE 6. Themes from classical sources dealing with doubt and the fidelity test, at key points in the plot

INITIAL SITUATION	▪ two friends, doubles, rivals ▪ two couples
INCITEMENT TO DOUBT	▪ praise/arousal of desire ▪ presence of an inciter ▪ presence of a facilitator-confidant; doubts about fidelity ▪ wager
TEST	▪ using deception to seduce ▪ disguise ▪ gifts and flattery ▪ hidden deception without seduction ▪ hidden husband
TEST RESULT	▪ surrender ▪ resistance ▪ husband's regret/revenge ▪ female disguise
FINAL SITUATION	▪ tragic ending ▪ happy ending 1: wife chooses new lover ▪ happy ending 2: original couples reunited

the truth, lies, hidden witnesses, and even violence. The result of the test is also expressed in different ways: There can be submission or resistance, regret and/or revenge, and escape in disguise. The ending, an essential part of any story, can be tragic or happy. It can sometimes even be happy at first, before suddenly turning tragic. If it does end happily, this happiness will only be partial, in that if it ends with the wife choosing her new lover, the husband will lose his beloved, and if it ends in reconciliation, the desire aroused in her by the new suitor will be left unfulfilled.

The next stages of the analysis involve identifying the main sources and examining whether the themes mentioned in the list appear in each source. This information is set out in Table 7, in which *Così fan tutte* is also analyzed for comparison purposes. The top row of the table shows the thematic motifs detected in all the sources, as identified in Table 6, while a selection of those sources are listed in the left-hand column. I begin with *Così fan tutte* to make it as easy as possible to compare it with the other works. After that, the sources are ranked according to the number of elements they share with *Così*. As far as possible, I have tried to group together those works with the greatest number of shared features. This table has two main objectives: first, to discover the relationship between the sources and the work I am studying, and second, to find possible associations between the different sources based on the presence or absence of a particular distinctive feature.

After a close scrutiny of Table 7, the following questions arise: What did Da Ponte take from these sources? And from which? First, all the sources coincide from the outset in establishing a rivalry between two men: In some cases, they are friends who end up being enemies, in others they meet by chance and begin competing out of envy, and sometimes although they do not actually meet, they end up fighting for the same object and thus become rivals. In *Così*, Ferrando and Guglielmo are presented as inseparable friends who are identical in everything, something that the libretto and the music insist on emphasizing.

The other element that appears in almost all the sources is the incitement of desire through excessive praise. That is to say, in these stories the authors considered it important to allow at least one of the male characters to publicly extol something that he believes is his possession. That something is always a woman, and what he is extolling is the certainty that this woman is his, and his alone. This action fuels the desire of the other member of the pair, and this feeds back into the extoller's own desire. This is what happens with Ferrando and Guglielmo, who begin the opera by taking turns at praising the fidelity of their fiancées. However, it is also important not to forget that Fiordiligi and Dorabella do the same, devoting their first scene to flattering descriptions of their beloveds.

These two elements of the plot, the male doubles in the initial situation and their public praise of their prized possessions, are absolutely essential, in that without them there would be no story. This creates the basis for the conflict, which is identical in all the sources: When two equals desire the same object, peace and harmony disappear. From this moment on, however, various differences between the stories begin to emerge.

The first difference is the double couple, which is almost exclusive to the libretto of *Così* and which, as already mentioned, is probably included as a device to allow the characters to interchange partners, a game popular

TABLE 7. Comparison of thematic motifs in *Così fan tutte* with those from classical sources

	INITIAL SITUATION		INCITEMENT TO DOUBT					TEST	
	Two friends; Doubles rivals	Two couples	Praise for; exciting; desire	Doubt inciter	Facilitator Confidant	Doubt about fidelity	Wager	Deceit for seducing	Disguise
Così fan tutte	X	X	X	DA; DP	DP; DA	(X)	X	X	X
Hyginus; *Fables*; **Ovid**; *Metamor-phoses*	X		X	goddess Aurora		X		X	X
Ariosto; *Orlando* 43; (Knight of Po)	X		X	sorceress Melissa		X		X	X
Cervantes; *Don Quijote*; (El curioso)	X		X	husband	Leonela	X		X	
Ariosto; *Orlando* 28	X	X							
Ariosto; *Orlando* 43; (Anselmo)	X			husband	Argia's maid	X			
Titus Livy; *History of Rome*; **Ovid**; *Fasti*	X		X		Lucretia's friend				
Boccaccio; *Decameron*	X		X	merchant Ambruog.	a poor woman	(X)	X		
Shake-speare; *Cymbeline*	X		X	Italian knight Iachimo		X	X		
Cervantes; *Don Quijote*; (Cardenio)	X	X	X		Dorotea's maid			X	

TEST (*continued*)			TEST RESULT				ENDING			CHARACTERS
Gifts and flatteries	Hidden deceit without seduction	Hidden husband	Claudication	Final resistance	Husband's lament/; revenge	Female scape/; disguise	Tragic ending	Happy ending 1: Adutery	Happy ending 2: Original couple	
X; flatt.		(GL witness)	X	FL's; intent	X	FL's; intent			X	Ferrando; Guglielmo; Dorabella Fiordiligi
X; gifts			X				2nd; X		1st; X	Cephalus; Cephalus in disguise; Procris
X; flatt.			X		X	X; scape		X		Knight of Po; Knight in disguise; Knight's wife
X; flatt.		X	X		X		2nd X	1st; X		Anselmo; Lotario; Camila
X; gifts		X	X						X	Astolfo; Iocondo; their wives
X; gifts			X		X; Kill order	X			X	Anselmo; Adonio; Argia
	X; rape			X			X			Collatinus; Tarquinius; Lucretia
	X; chest; &; lie			X	X; Kill order	X; disguise			X	Bernabò; Ambruogiuolo; Zinevra
	X; chest; &; lie			X	X; Kill order	X; disguise			X	Leonatus; Iachimo; Imogen
X; Dor-otea		X; Lus-cinda	X; Dorotea	X; Luscinda					X	Cardenio; Fernando; Luscinda; Dorotea

in many eighteenth-century comedies. The next element is the doubt about their sweetheart's fidelity that gives rise to the test. Doubt as such is only made explicit in the characters of Cephalus, the Knight of the Po, the two Anselmos, and Leonatus. The rest of the male protagonists, including Ferrando and Guglielmo in *Così*, claim to have no doubts. However, they agree to submit their beloveds to the test, so that in the end they are also accepting the possibility of failure. Only Rinaldo, in refusing to drink from the cup, demonstrates the common sense that all the others lack and that they will belatedly acquire once they have undergone the testing experience.

The way doubt arises could be seen as another difference. It either germinates within the subject's own head (often the husband, as in the two Anselmos), or it arises due to the agency of another character who sows suspicion in the subject's mind. The latter option is the most frequent and is also the one chosen by Da Ponte. By mocking his two friends' faith in their lovers, Don Alfonso manages to plant the shadow of suspicion, in much the same way as the goddess Aurora, the sorceress Melissa, the merchant Ambrogiuolo, and the knight Iachimo. It is important to remember, however, that the seed had already been planted with the initial flattery of the possessed object.

Next is the test itself. In *Così*, the preliminary step before holding the test is the acceptance of a wager. In the sources, the only two stories in which specific mention is made of a wager with money or jewels are the *Decameron* and *Cymbeline*. These two works fall within the group of stories in which there is no seduction, and instead what we have is deception or even rape, with the woman resisting until the end. They are exceptions within the tradition of doubt and fidelity test stories, and seem to originate from the tale of Lucretia as narrated by Livy and Ovid. This means the wager is only found in stories that involve coercion and resistance instead of seduction and yielding. Da Ponte blends the two: He includes the motif of the wager, taken directly from Boccaccio or perhaps Shakespeare, and also coincides with those sources in the happy ending that reunites the original couples, a conclusion that departs from the classical tale. However, *Così* differs from Boccaccio and Shakespeare's tales in the other main aspect, the process of seduction during the test, in which flattery or gifts from a disguised suitor causes the woman to succumb to his charms. Thus, the story of doubts and unfulfilled desires offers two options to the author telling the tale of the test, either seduction and yielding or coercion and resistance. Although Da Ponte borrows the idea of the wager from the coercion and resistance version of the test, he clearly prefers the seduction and yielding option, in that he carefully explores the mechanisms of a deliberate, premeditated fidelity test and sets out its likely consequences.[30]

The dilemmas explored in *Così fan tutte* are resolved in a double ending. The first ending comes with the result of the test. The "Albanians" successfully seduce Dorabella and Fiordiligi before revealing that they are in fact Ferrando and Guglielmo. This painful revelation of the truth triggers in the characters a whole array of feelings, of horror, humiliation, indignation, and a desire for revenge. Fortunately, these are followed by a second set of calmer, more composed reactions, which eventually allow the antagonists to settle their differences and make up. Forgiveness and prudence emerge as the most desirable virtues. Once again, Da Ponte opts for the most popular ending in the sources, in which the original couples are given a second chance, now much the wiser after witnessing how foolish it is to deny human fragility and put it to the test. The only exceptions are *El curioso impertinente* and the story of the Knight of the Po, whose protagonists are denied this second chance, condemning them to lose their prized treasures forever, as a punishment for their foolishness.

In this chapter, the aim has been to gather together and analyze the possible sources of the libretto of *Così*. These sources must contain all, or almost all, of the ingredients that come together in this opera. To this end, I have carefully examined the details of the different stories, isolating the various thematic elements of which they are composed. By observing and comparing these elements, I have come to several conclusions. First, all the sources, despite their differences, tell the same story, structured around the same five stages: the initial situation, the incitement to doubt and desire, the fidelity test, the outcome of the test, and the final situation. Most of them also coincide in making the main conflict in the plot arise from a rivalry between doubles and the incitement of desire by praising the object. In fact, the differences between the sources and *Così fan tutte* center around minor motifs, such as the double couples, which are almost exclusive to *Così* and whose presence does not affect the revelation of the laws of mimetic desire—and, if anything, makes it even clearer. Another difference is the wager. Curiously, it only appears in the sources in which the heroines resist seduction, which is not the case in *Così*. It is possible that Da Ponte added this motif simply because it made his male characters more credible, so allowing him to emphasize the impetuous, frivolous character of the two young friends.

To summarize, it is evident that Da Ponte created an original mixture when composing the libretto of *Così*, drawing on Ariosto (43, the story of the Knight of the Po) and Cervantes (*El curioso impertinente*) in the initial situation and subsequent development of the story, and Shakespeare and Boccaccio in the wager theme, before culminating the dramatic action with a happy ending typical of the comedy genre. However, this ending also has a serious message, in that although the original couples get back together at the end, they are quite different from the naïve, romantic couples presented at the beginning: They are wiser and more aware of their weaknesses—in short, more human.

CHAPTER 4

The Novelistic Truth about the Mechanisms of Desire

Before continuing with the study of *Così*, I should perhaps pause to explain the principles on which my analysis of the opera is based, namely the mimetic theory of the French philosopher René Girard, which he presented and developed in a multitude of publications over the course of fifty years. This theory has contributed to a radical transformation of disciplines as diverse as literary criticism, anthropology, economics, and theology. This would suggest it could also provide the basis for a new approach to the analysis of certain operas, which in essence are works of theater.

In this section, I will explain the part of Girard's theory that serves as a basis for the analysis proposed here—in other words his hypothesis on mimetic desire and its revelation in literary works, especially in novels and plays.[1] Girard went on to make various other discoveries, such as humanity's use of the scapegoat mechanism as an ancient solution to the mimetic rivalry that leads to mutual destruction, and the defense of the victim's innocence that reveals the lie behind the notion of sacrifice, the cornerstone of Christian revelation. Although these are fundamental aspects for those wishing to gain a full understanding of Girard's theory, I will not be analyzing them in great detail here, as they do not feature in *Così fan tutte*.

Let's begin with a basic principle: The human being "seeks to make himself a being who is essentially founded on his fellow being's desire."[2] This means imitating other people's desires, mimesis, is an inherent feature of the human species: "In human relations mimesis is the dominant factor."[3] In fact, this is precisely what humanizes, or what differentiates the human species from animals. Girard distinguishes between the "appetite felt for food or sex," a "merely biological matter," and "desire," which appears "when the imitation of a model comes into play."[4] Contrary to what we think, our desires are neither original nor spontaneous, but are always imitations of the desires of others. We experience desire for an object because we observe that desire in another person and we copy it. A triangular relationship is thus established between the subject, the object and the model or mediator, a relationship that Girard calls "external" when subject and model are physically or temporally distant, and "internal" when they are close. This is an important difference, because the closer the subject is to the model, the more intense the rivalry that arises between them, a natural consequence of imitative desire. If we imitate another person's desire for a particular object, we will tend to consider that person as a rival, an obstacle. The more the person resembles us, the closer they are to us, the greater this rivalry will become.

Here are two examples from the classics of literature studied by Girard: Don Quijote longs to achieve the fame enjoyed by Amadis de Gaulle, but the distance between him and his model is so huge that he could never consider him a rival. By contrast, in Stendhal's *Le rouge et le noir*, the mayor of Verrières, M. Rênal, wishes to engage Julien Sorel as a tutor to his children because he thinks that his rich neighbor Valenod also wants Sorel for this job. Although the desire the mayor is copying is in fact imaginary, for him it is real, and this desire grows within him in the same proportion as his rivalry with his neighbor, who becomes an obstacle for him.[5] Vanity, envy, jealousy, and hate, which in itself requires a blend of veneration and resentment, are terms that ultimately refer to the same phenomenon: when a subject becomes fixated on a model whose desire they copy, so converting them into antagonists.

This mimetic mechanism can be unleashed at any moment "and with the appearance of literally anyone."[6] In this case the subject freely makes their own decision and in fact "chooses the model rather than the object,"[7]—in other words, they choose to "be" the model through the acquisition of the object, for "All desire is desire to be."[8] It is "metaphysical desire":

> Once his primordial needs are satisfied, and sometimes even before, man desires intensely, but he does not know exactly what, for it is the being that he desires, a being he feels deprived of and which another man seems to him to be endowed with. The subject waits for this other man to tell him what he should desire if he wishes to acquire this being.[9]

This desire can also be stimulated, for example, by the model singing the praises—of the object: In *El curioso impertinente*, when Anselmo extols the virtues of his beloved in front of his friend Lothario, he arouses in him the desire to possess her, so that what was at first a feigned passion later becomes real.[10] In *Così*, both the two friends and the two sisters proclaim to their doubles the numerous qualities of their lovers, thereby arousing in them envy or desire for the object possessed by the other. Desire can also be kindled via rejection, especially when the subject perceives this rejection as an obstacle on their quest to secure what they desires. In the same way, desire can be extinguished once the desired object is finally attained. In *Don Quijote*, Altisidora "feigns a passion for Don Quijote but is genuinely angered when she is spurned by him"; this rejection causes real desires to be born within her.[11] At the beginning of *Così fan tutte*, the two friends feel secure about their respective possessions and show no desire for anyone else; the fire is lit by Don Alfonso's doubts about the sisters' fidelity and, once the seduction game begins, the women's rejections of their pretend lovers only redouble the men's desire.

Once established, the rivalry is transferred or spread to the model, who then imitates the desire of the subject, who in turn becomes a model for their rival's desire. In other words, when the model becomes aware of the subject's desire for their prized possession, this only serves to magnify their desire for that same possession: "That desire which is yours and which I am going to imitate, may well have been insignificant at the beginning, and may perhaps have lacked any strong intensity. But, when I move towards the same object as you, the intensity of your desire increases."[12] During the ensuing dispute, they come to forget the object over which their rivalry first appeared:

> In other words, it always evolves towards more reciprocity, and therefore towards more conflict. This is what I call a relationship of doubles. In the crossfire of rivalry, the object disappears; very soon, the sole obsession of

> the two rivals is to defeat the opponent, rather than to obtain the object. Obtaining the object becomes a mere pretext for exacerbating the conflict. The rivals become more and more identical to each other, they become doubles of each other. The mimetic crisis is always a crisis of undifferentiation.[13]

Therefore, internal mediation gives way to undifferentiation, to the disappearance of the differences between the competing doubles due to their focus on their rivalry and the disappearance of the object. This rivalry immediately spreads by mimetic contagion to other subjects, so that in the end they reach a point of rivalry of "all against all."

> If two people come to blows over the same object, its value increases in the eyes of a third party who is observing the striking display of rivalry; or, in other words, the object of desire exerts its seductive powers over an increasing number of individuals, focusing them around itself. When the rival's mimetic attraction grows, the object at the origin of the conflict tends progressively to fade away, . . . it breaks up, it is destroyed, in the midst of the huge fight between all those competing for it. . . . When this happens, doubles proliferate, and the mimetic crisis spreads and intensifies more and more.[14]

This situation of total rivalry leads inevitably to the self-destruction of the group. It is impossible for the group to start reasoning and discover that it is a victim of collective contagion. The worst thing of all is that the group does not actually realize that it has been infected; in other words, both the individual and the group are unaware that their desires are a copy of the desires of others. They think that their rivalries and desires are original, unique, and justified, when the truth is that they have been copied and transferred. Girard calls this factor *méconnaissance* (unknowing or misrecognition), which is not the same as the Freudian unconscious, as there is no deterministic force acting on the self. Unknowing is the situation of the individual, or the group, which is immersed in mutual violence, unaware that it is suffering from the mimetic disease.

Faced, therefore, with the prospect of total destruction, the group discovers a mechanism that can save it: It focuses all its anger against a single member, so that the "all against all" becomes "all against one." That one, who cannot possibly win such an unequal fight, is branded the cause of all this disorder; the blame is heaped upon them, to the point that they themself admit their guilt, before being killed, sacrificed by the masses. The sacrifice of this scapegoat brings momentary peace, until a new mimetic conflict is unleashed. The periodic repetition of the sacrifice or the remembrance of it becomes a ritual for the community, ensuring peaceful coexistence in the face of inevitable outbreaks of violence. Girard's theory delves deeper, entering the field of myths, rites, and sacred texts, especially the Bible, to reach very interesting findings that help explain the prevalence of violence within human societies, its relationship with the sacred, and the role played in the history of humankind by "the Christian revelation of the fundamental innocence of the victims."[15] However, as mentioned earlier, these go far beyond the scope of this study, in which I focus on the specific question of mimetic desire and how it is revealed in literature, theater, and, by extension, opera.

Literature as a Special Place for Revealing Mimetic Desire

Girard first began to intuit the fundamental role of mimetic desire in human relationships during an intensive period of study of nineteenth-century French literature for a course he was to teach at Indiana University. These intuitions crystallized in his first book, *Mensonge romantique et vérité romanesque*, published in 1961. Other books followed, in which he probed deeper into the study of mimetic revelation in the works of several well-known authors: *Proust: A Collection of Critical Essays* (1962), *Dostoïevski. Du double à l'unité* (1963), *Critiques dans un souterrain* (1976), "*To Double Business Bound*": *Essays on Literature, Mimesis and Anthropology* (1978), and *A Theater of Envy: William Shakespeare* (1991).[16] This culminated in 2010 with *Géometries du désir*, a compilation of his previously published studies on literary themes.[17]

By approaching works of literature "as is," without preconceived ideas or prejudices and assuming them to be bearers of truth, Girard found that "certain exceptional works (not literature as such)" are "agents of a very special demystification": that bears on the "hidden role of mimetic effects in human interaction."[18] He confirmed that "the only texts that have ever discovered mimetic desire and explored some of its consequences are literary texts."[19] According to Girard, these works, or rather their authors, revealed that the conflicts between human beings arise out of mimetic disease, from the impulse of mimetic desire. On numerous occasions throughout their works, these authors tried to make this clear via the reactions of their characters. In other words, novelists and playwrights such as Dante, Cervantes, Shakespeare, Marivaux, Stendhal, Fyodor Dostoevsky, Gustave Flaubert, Marcel Proust, and Albert Camus, among others, came to perceive the crucial role of mimetic desire in human nature, to such an extent that their works are a systematic exploration of this mechanism. The relationships between their characters become conflictual because of the rivalry born of desire, which is always mimetic, and this rivalry leads to violence and very often to tragedy.

Girard's new vision of literature obliged him to confront a prejudice that was deeply rooted in literary studies and first appeared in the Romantic period: the claim that each literary work represents an original, spontaneous thought, which can only be interpreted in the light of that spontaneity. In fact, this vision is inherent to a reader who, "generally convinced of his own spontaneity, projects onto the work the meanings that he already projects onto the world."[20] Instead, Girard looked for the similarities between the texts, rather than the differences: "I have understood that what critics have always scorned in novels—the recurrence of fascination and jealousy, the reciprocal manipulations, the lies to the other and to oneself, etc. . . . Everything that repels due to its repetitive nature . . . are the fundamental maneuvers and the ruses of mimetic desire."[21] In this way, he found that by exposing human conflicts due to rivalries between subject, object, and mediator, certain works strove to reveal the mediator's presence, while others merely reflected their presence but "without ever revealing it."[22] He adjectivized the former works as "novelistic" (*romanesques*) and the latter as "romantic" (*romantiques*), and concluded that, while novelistic works allow us to discover the truth about human behaviors and what really motivates us to act the way we do, something that usually remains hidden from "the common view,"[23]—romantic works do nothing more than replicate the lie perpetuated by hiding the truth. He therefore contrasted the "novelistic truth" (*vérité romanesque*) of certain works with the "romantic lie" (*mensonge romantique*) of others.

In line with these findings, Girard went so far as to defend the scientific role played by literary criticism in anthropological studies, by launching an attack against those who denied "any real investigative power to a literary work."[24] This thesis was later reinforced by Cesáreo Bandera, when he talked about the intertextuality of literary texts in relation to the sources of the libretto of *Così*. Bandera stated that "nothing essential separates literature from other cultural phenomena. . . . This enables us to argue that everything is like literary fiction and that literary fiction is like everything else."[25] In other words, the fictional nature of the events presented does not invalidate literary fiction as a producer of truth. Literature in general, and novels and plays in particular, is an excellent vehicle for representing mimetic desire and for revealing the mechanism behind it, which is normally hidden from view. According to Girard, the authors' intuition can be explained by analyzing these works in their literality, setting aside any previous methodologies, in order to unravel "the paradoxical but logical network of mimetic entanglements spun by the great literary works."[26] It is as if the novel were unveiling the mechanics of desire to us.

One of the keys enabling us to distinguish between novelistic truth and romantic lie can be found in the endings. Only when the character discovers that they have suffered the "disease" of mimetic desire can they really begin to be cured of it. In the denouement, the protagonist contemplates the ravages left behind by this mimetic desire and becomes aware of their "ontological disease." This is what happens to Don Quijote, who dies sane, lucid, and conscious, cured by the pen of Cervantes; and to the characters in *A Midsummer Night's Dream*, who wake up believing they have lived through an endless series of nightmares. The same thing happens to the double couples in *Così*, who are reconciled half ashamed, half repentant, in the firm conviction that "it is better not to do the test." In many cases, however, all the characters can do is to helplessly survey the absurdity of an unrestrained violence that leads to total annihilation (*Romeo and Juliet*, *Hamlet*, *Othello*, *Madame Bovary*). In all these stories, comic or tragic, in the end it is the readers or the audience who obtain the cure for the disease, in that the hidden truth about the destructive power of desires is revealed to them in the pages of the novel or in the action that takes place on stage. This was at least how Girard understood it, one of whose merits, in my opinion, is to have approached the texts from the perspective of an unprejudiced reader. By taking this radical new approach to literary criticism, in which he effectively declared himself independent of possible models or rivals, he was himself renouncing the opportunity to imitate his peers and share in their prestige.

The Novelistic Truth of the Opera Genre

As he explored the different literary genres, Girard found that mimetic desire reveals itself most intensely in theatrical works. In fact, his theory of triangular desire seems to be particularly well suited to the theatrical genre, in that it requires the spatial dimensions between the mediator, subject, and object to be defined, and space in the theater is a basic factor. It could be argued, paraphrasing one of the scholars of Girard's work, that the triangle of desire could be regarded as theatrical: "The addition of the mediator to the dual subject-object relationship adds a second dimension that defines a space—certainly still metaphorical—for desire."[27] And what is so special about theatrical representation, about the staging of a story? In theater, life can be imitated in a very convincing way because, in the absence of a narrator, everything we know is obtained through the characters' words, gestures, and actions. These are the same limitations we experience in everyday human life, and perhaps that is why we find theatrical fiction so fascinating and attractive. We are hidden guests, voyeurs in front of whom the drama unfolds, without a narrator to provide additional clues or information.

If we add music to the play, opera is born. It is drama in which the action takes place musically. Operas are, in essence, theatrical works that are sung, plays set to music. The events take place in an unreal, fictional world in which everyone expresses themselves through music. As spectators we are prepared a priori to accept this fictional world of music, even before we accept the fiction of the drama itself. Once we take our seats, the curtain rises, and we enter this musical world, the opera recovers its dramatic power as a work of theater and as such can also reveal the human laws that govern desire.

Unfortunately, Girard did not publish any studies on opera. In a review of his books and interviews, I found just two direct references to the operatic genre. The first comes from a conversation between Girard and the stage designer Philippe Godefroid, an extract of which was published in 1985 in the French opera magazine *L'Avant scène opéra.*[28] During this conversation, the two men discuss the relationship between opera and myth. The published version contains what appear to be Girard's words transcribed by Godefroid, since the text is simply entitled "Entretien avec René Girard" (Meeting with René Girard), and he is not cited as the author. Girard looks at two operas in particular: *Don Giovanni* by Mozart and *The Ring of the Nibelung* by Richard Wagner. When looking for the sense of myth in *Don Giovanni,* Girard directs our gaze towards the reactions of the characters surrounding Don Giovanni rather than towards the death of the hero, always traditionally interpreted in a heroic tone. He is more interested in what he calls the "collective elements": the complicity between the three women, the final quintet that underlines the recovery of the established order after Don Giovanni's death, and, especially, the organization of the couples, the game of doubles, "in which identity is less important than rivalry." To support his point of view, Girard recalls that in *Così fan tutte* and *Le nozze di Figaro* we also find that the pairings are not part of some immutable order and that "it is enough to disguise oneself, or to hide oneself, to shuffle the cards in a different way, for hearts to start beating differently."[29] He criticizes, as he had done in *Mensonge romantique*, the erroneous interpretation of the myth that emerged in the nineteenth century. By erasing "the mimetic discourse and the collective violence" and placing all the emphasis on Don Giovanni's resistance and death, and on the Commendatore as a kind of avenging god, that interpretation disguised and completely modified "the true problematic" expressed in the play. As regards *The Ring*, Girard is convinced that, at least in the first of the operas, *The Rhine Gold*, "a reading by means of mimetic desire is evident," since the whole work "is built entirely on the mechanisms of desire and doubles."[30]

This brief article is valuable both for its exceptionality within Girard's work and for the ideas presented. It is also very interesting that in 1985 Girard would have been asked by an opera specialist such as Godefroid (still very young at the time, but who would become an expert in Wagnerian productions) to offer his opinions on the relationship between opera, myth, and mimetic desire in a specialized medium. Godefroid introduces Girard simply as a "researcher and professor at Stanford University" and not as the great intellectual he would later be known as. His appearance in *L'Avant scène* is probably due to the fact that Godefroid already regarded Girard as one of his main influences as an artist and researcher, so that his 1985 "entretien" may have been a personal and isolated attempt to give voice to Girard's theory.[31] It is also striking that Girard's ideas could be accepted into the musicological debate with such remarkable ease. Experts came to seek him out, as on so many other occasions, and listened to him attentively. Unfortunately, this analysis covered just two pages of reflections, published in a specialized media rather than in a book aimed at the general public. In any case, it is a shame that this brief incursion into music did not continue and that Girard's revolutionary approach to literature has not been transferred in some way to music.

The second direct source regarding opera's relationship with mimetic theory consists of a brief reference put forward by Girard as an example during conversations with Michel Treguer published in 1994 in *Quand ces choses commenceront*. When asked about how the same human relationships can be found in literature as in real life, Girard mentioned various cases that he considered "almost too obvious."[32] First he cites *Carmen*, in which he claimed desire increased in the face of obstacle and rejection, so provoking the tragic ending. Girard is referring to, without explicitly mentioning it, Prosper Mérimée's novel (1847) rather than Georges Bizet's opera (1875), although mimetic desire plays the same role in both versions. A little later he offers another "obvious" example, this time from an opera, focusing again on Wagner's *Ring of the Nibelung*. Girard points out that the opening scene of *The Rhine Gold*, which revolves around the value of the gold guarded by the Rhinemaidens, reveals that the fascination for the object has nothing to do with the object itself ("the gold is nothing") and instead "it is the fact of disputing it that gives it its value."[33] For Girard this beginning is "visionary," and he exclaims: "It is that of Marivaux, it is also that of Shakespeare!"[34] These brief comments make no reference to the music and the entire focus is on the actions and words set out in the libretto. What is interesting, however, is that Girard could draw on examples from operas as naturally as he did from plays and novels. This shows that for him there was no difference between the various genres when seeking the novelistic truth, and the fact that he did not study any particular opera in depth does not mean he rejected the genre as a producer of truth. In conclusion, although in my exploration of *Così* from the perspective of Girard's ideas, I cannot base my research on his musical analyses, I can still be confident that he would have approved of my choice of subject. And in any case, his observant studies of theatrical works, such as Shakespeare's plays, are an essential guide for the analysis of the operas that later adopted those works as librettos.[35]

If we look beyond Girard himself to the scholars who devote their research to his theory, I have found just five texts in which opera is directly related to mimetic theory. All five are brief articles or dissertations. The earliest two, from 1985, are also by Godefroid and were published in the same issue of the magazine *L'Avant scène opéra* in which his "meeting" with Girard was recounted. They are very concise, barely two pages each. The first discusses Wagner from the perspective of Girard's theory, while the second offers a more concrete study of the role of the designated victim and of the mimetic game in his opera *The Flying Dutchman*.[36]

The third, more recent article is by Berry Vorstenbosch, who studied the way in which the scapegoat mechanism is revealed in Modest Mussorgsky's opera *Boris Godunov* (premiered in 1874, with a libretto based on the drama of the same name by Alexander Pushkin).[37] I found Vorstenbosch's starting point very interesting, so much so that it inspired my own approach to Mozart's opera. He does not set out to prove that *Boris Godunov* is a case in which mimetic theory applies, but rather that the study of this work can provide a better understanding of mimetic theory. In this way, taking a similar line to Girard himself, he tries to allow the opera to tell its own truth by observing it without prejudging it in any way. However, his analysis centers on the libretto (the actions, the words, the gestures), and he pays little attention to the music.

The remaining two references linking opera and mimetic theory are more recent, though less direct. The first is a doctoral dissertation from the University of Pennsylvania by Daniel Villegas,[38] devoted to the study of mimesis, or more specifically, "mimetology," in "early modern opera." Unfortunately for my purposes, it does not deal with any specific work in depth, and his philosophical outlook forces him to center his research on characters, actions, and words rather than on music. In short, he moves away from the approach endorsed by Girard and Godefroid, and is therefore of little help here. The last text is by Benoît Chantre, a personal friend of Girard, who in 2016 published a book entitled *Les derniers jours de René Girard*.[39] This ambiguous title refers both to the end of the thinker's life and to his apocalyptic vision as to the direction in which our world was heading. Inside, Chantre offers his own analyses of the theory of desire in literary works, paying particular attention to the myth of Don Juan, especially in Mozart and Da Ponte's opera *Don Giovanni*. Once again, however, we find that the music is not analyzed, and that the author concentrates exclusively on the characters' actions and words.

In conclusion, it would seem that musical works, and more specifically operas, could be analyzed from the perspective of mimetic theory in much the same way as Girard analyzed literature. So far, very little research has been done in this direction. The few timid incursions into this field have had no clearly defined objectives and have focused mainly on the literary aspects, that is the libretto, rather than on the music. In fact, none of the studies I found contains extracts from the music. If we compare this to the vast, ever-growing Girardian bibliography on literary works, films, and soon maybe video games, the almost complete absence of studies on specific operas from the point of view of Girard's theory might probably discourage us from advancing any further. Why has so little research been done in this direction? Perhaps because the music, which from Mozart onwards has been considered the master of the poetry rather than the servant,[40] tends to impose itself on the text set out in the libretto, making its interpretation more difficult? Or perhaps because the presence of music in opera might discourage the uninitiated from venturing into this field, or simply because few musicologists are familiar with Girard's theory? Whatever the reason, I personally am convinced that the truth about the laws of mimetic desire has also been expressed in opera, as shown by the few examples that Girard himself put forward, some of which referred to Mozart. The case of *Così fan tutte*, moreover, brings together two encouraging signs: a plot based on sources that have themselves been studied from the perspective of mimetic desire, and the repeated misunderstanding, or even rejection of its libretto in the nineteenth century, when the romantic lie held sway.

The next obstacle to overcome is how to find the hidden truth in a work that was published in two separate volumes, libretto and score. Most operas require at least two creators,[41] each responsible for a different form of expression: One provides the script (the words, actions, and gestures used by the performers), and the other provides the music. On some occasions they collaborate, working together in the same direction, while on others they contradict, taunt, or mock each other. For the viewer, the result is normally a single, comprehensible whole, but for the researcher the challenge is to find out how the two forms of expression combine and work together.[42] This is what I intend to do in the next chapter.

CHAPTER 5

Mimetic Revelation in *Così fan tutte*

DOUBLES HAVE BEEN A POPULAR DEVICE THROUGHOUT THE HISTORY of literature. I have already mentioned some of them in my review of the classical sources of the libretto of *Così fan tutte*: Collatinus and Tarquinius (in *History of Rome* 1.58–60 by Livy and in *Fasti* 2.725–834 by Ovid), Cloridano and Medoro (in *Orlando* 1.18–19), Astolfo and Iocondo (in *Orlando* 2.28), Anselmo and Adonio (in *Orlando* 2.43), Anselmo and Lothario (in *Don Quijote* 1.33–35), and Fernando and Cardenio (in *Don Quijote* 1.24, 27–29, 36). In all these cases, when the reader is introduced to the pair of friends, there are two recurring elements: the great similarity or closeness between the two members of the pair, and the author's insistence on making this clear from the very beginning. In Cervantes's *El curioso impertinente*, for example, there is a close friendship between the two friends Anselmo and Lothario, and strong mutual admiration. For Girard there is no doubt that "Cervantes insists extensively, at the beginning of his story, on the friendship that unites the two protagonists."[1] However, this friendship, which is described as a total identification of feelings, attitudes, and tastes, is accompanied "by an acute feeling of rivalry" that "remains in the shadows."[2] Girard observes that the identification, or the extreme similarity, between the two friends is an essential ingredient of the story to help us understand that the two men who will later become rivals are very close when the story begins. This situation is highlighted by Girard several times in his literary analyses, in works such as Cervantes's *El curioso impertinente*, in Dostoevsky's *The Eternal Husband*, or in the episode about Paolo and Francesca from Dante's *The Divine Comedy*.[3] In all these cases, "the nearer the mediator, the more does the veneration that he inspires give way to hate and rivalry," "A Paolo who encountered Lancelot every day would no doubt prefer Queen Guinevere to Francesca, unless he managed to link Francesca and his rival, making the rival desire her, so as to desire her the more himself—to desire her *through* him or rather against him."[4] This closeness or "internal mediation" is an essential condition for the desire of appropriation, the mimetic desire, to arise between the doubles. This is exactly the situation we find in *Così fan tutte*. At the beginning of the opera, the authors go to great strides to show the identification between Ferrando and Guglielmo and between Fiordiligi and Dorabella, a sine qua non to enable internal mediation to take place between them. This is achieved, as we will soon see, by literary, dramatic, and, especially, musical techniques.

In some cases, what Girard defines as "double mediation" can also be achieved, in that desire can rapidly travel from subject to mediator and from mediator to subject, so that "two identical triangles running in opposite directions overlap each other. Desire circulates more and more quickly between the two rivals, increasing in intensity with each exchange."[5] "In double mediation," Girard states, "one doesn't desire the object as much as one fears seeing it possessed by someone else."[6] Indeed, throughout *Così* we see how desire spreads contagiously between the two friends. In order to claim their rival's prized possession, the doubles first act together (in act 1) and then separately (in act 2). When Ferrando moves in on Guglielmo's possession, Guglielmo approaches Ferrando's possession, and vice versa. In fact, when Ferrando discovers that Guglielmo has managed to steal Dorabella from him, he redoubles his efforts to win Fiordiligi's heart. Do they both fear losing their betrothed? Of course they do, even though they deny it to Don Alfonso, or they would never have accepted the wager. Do they both set out on a race to dispossess their rival? Once again, the answer is yes. And the same is true of Fiordiligi and Dorabella, who begin act 1 seemingly united in their desire for their beloveds and end up imitating each other in their attitudes towards their new suitors throughout act 2. When Dorabella finally confesses to Fiordiligi her desire for her new love, Fiordiligi in turn decides to yield to her own feelings. In other words, from internal mediation we have moved on to double mediation, both of which figure highly in *Così fan tutte*.

Consider for a moment the object of desire of the doubles in this opera. In this case there is not just one object, but two, albeit identical and interchangeable: Fiordiligi and Dorabella are interchangeable, as are the two "Albanians." According to Girard, the object of desire is of no importance in itself, in that it could easily be exchanged for some other object, as long as this object is also the product of a mimetic desire. It is remarkable that Kunze, who seems to have been completely unaware of Girard's theory, expressly highlighted this issue of the interchangeability of the object of each character's desire as a crucial aspect of his analysis of the opera. In his opinion, "*Così fan tutte* is a work about . . . the problem of identity and interchangeability . . . love is transferable and its objects are interchangeable, so that the individual is substitutable.[7] Later, he returns to this same idea: "Only in *Così fan tutte* does this ancient comic motif of identity supplantation become a major theme. It reaches threatening dimensions, because it endangers and even destroys human society . . . permutation should not be regarded as just one of many elements of the comic play. It is the theme and the hypothesis that must be demonstrated."[8] The loss of identity, or the equalization and interchangeability of the characters, is a threat to order, the origin of chaos. The degree to which this author's interpretations coincide with those of Girard is quite astonishing.[9]

The question now is to discover how music can express the identity of the doubles, the first step towards achieving internal and double mediation. It can do so through joint singing, in other words through the various ways of juxtaposing the singing of the two characters. The fact that two characters share the same strong feelings can be manifested in music in two ways: by identical melodic repetitions in alternate imitative singing and by singing the same identical melodies together in a homophonic duet. Regardless of which option is chosen, the audience receive the same clear message: that the two characters have identical feelings and that imitation of their desire could easily spring from the imitation of their singing. That the two characters are singing exactly the same music is not supposed to produce scorn or derision, and it is not an attempt to make us laugh[10]; instead it is the music's way of making us experience the identity of feelings. Opposing feelings can also be expressed by melodic repetitions or by joint singing in much the same way.

Here, the differences between them are emphasized in the words they are singing. In this way, two exact opposites are created.

Music expresses this shared identity at the beginning of *Così fan tutte*. This is plain for all to see from the way the doubles or same-sex pairs convey themselves musically in the scenes in which they appear for the first time, namely in scene 1 for the male pair and scene 2 for the female pair. The *duettino* between Ferrando and Guglielmo from scene 4 should also be included because of its undeniable links with the earlier female duet. My analysis will therefore begin by focusing on the three tercets that make up the *introduzione* and the two duets in scenes 2 and 4 respectively.

Scene 1, which begins immediately after the Overture in C Major, is a sequence of three numbers—three terzettos or trios, separated by recitatives, which complete with their tonalities the triad of the work's tonic (G, E, C). In the first terzetto, "La mia Dorabella," the doubles, who sing to an identical melody, differ only in their tessitura, as Ferrando is a tenor while Guglielmo is a baritone. The bass voice of Don Alfonso completes the trio. The terzetto begins, in line with established convention, with the soloists' separate entrances (bars 8–29). This is followed by alternating voices (bars 29–43) and concludes with joint singing (bars 43–57). In the first part, the three characters also intervene separately : Ferrando proudly praises Dorabella's fidelity and beauty (bars 8–14); Guglielmo does likewise for Fiordiligi, singing to the same melody used by Ferrando (bars 14–22); and finally, Don Alfonso claims that he is right, "ex cathedra parlo" (I speak ex cathedra), although the audience still does not know what he is talking about (bars 22–29). The whole passage is heard, thanks to the harmony, as a closed, complete entity in itself, as it advances from the tonic G (Ferrando) to the dominant D (Guglielmo) before finally returning to the tonic G (Don Alfonso).

In the second part of the terzetto (bars 29–43), we hear the two friends singing alternately, followed by a response from Don Alfonso. They ask Don Alfonso, with identical, parallel musical parts, to prove what he has just said (that their lovers might be unfaithful, we now know). He advises them not to do the test ("Tai prove lasciamo"—Let us leave the tests), with an affirmative musical phrase that runs along the chord of D major, the dominant chord of the tonality. The doubles react ("No, no, le vogliamo"—No, no, we want them) by repeating the same melodic phrase used by Don Alfonso, in unison at octave distance but resolving on the tonic chord, a means of expressing

EXAMPLE 1. Bars 35–38, terzetto "La mia Dorabella," act 1, scene 1, no. 1

their determination. They continue singing together, now at a distance of a third (always at the octave), affirming three times that they are ready to use violence if necessary ("o fuori la spada"—or we draw the sword). Mozart parodically underlines the excessiveness of the soldiers' gesture by playing a fast, forte ascending scale on the violins just as they are singing the word "spada" (bars 35–38, Example 1). The fact that this gesture is exaggerated and out of place is also highlighted by not using the expected note, using its lower octave instead. As a result of all this, the audience now understands unequivocally that the two friends are united in their response and that it is definitive.

The game of alternate singing continues in a series of asides, before leading to the final joint singing of the third part. Up to this point, those following the sung text can clearly perceive that Ferrando and Guglielmo are united in their wish to test the fidelity of their lovers, despite the opposition of Don Alfonso, who believes it would be wiser not to do so.

In the last part of the terzetto (bars 43–57), the three voices sing in a very similar way, almost homophonically. However, the audience realizes there are two positions rather than three, thanks to the text, in which Ferrando and Guglielmo sing exactly the same text together, while Don Alfonso defends a completely opposite position. Thus, while Ferrando and Guglielmo display their wounded pride, with the doubts cast about the fidelity of their treasured possessions kindling in them the desire to put them to the test, Don Alfonso is convinced that any attempt to discover an evil that will destroy us is a "pazzo desire" (a mad desire). This debate is also attended by the audience, who, as events unfold, will have to decide which of the two sides was right.

In the recitative that links this first terzetto with the next one, Don Alfonso exposes the two young men to the harsh reality that their sweethearts are human. By taking the women off the divine pedestal on which the men had placed them and bringing them back down to earth, Don Alfonso is preparing us for a full denial of the romantic ideal in amorous desire. First, he replies to the enraged Ferrando that instead of invoking heaven with oaths, he, Don Alfonso, prefers to swear "alla terra" (to the earth). He then asks them whether their fiancés are goddesses or women. The doubles respond immediately: "Son donne" (They are women) (bars 19–21, Example 2). This answer is homophonic, reflecting their same initial opinion. They are under no illusions; they know they are women. However, the melody interspersed with silences, the unusual augmented fourth interval in Ferrando's part, the timid and slightly dreamy objections that the two men raise in the face of Don Alfonso's stern realism ("ma . . . son tali, son tali"—literally "but . . . they are such, they are such"), and, above all, the way the melody unravels the dominant chord of the tone, which remains unresolved, indicates that the men's identical adoration of their beloveds, however sincere it may seem, is empty, undefined, and incomplete. The vagueness of the word "tali" is emphasized by the ellipsis and by the fact that "tali" (such) is not followed by anything.[11] This is also transmitted by musical devices, such as the silences, the ascending melody, the augmented fourth interval, and the dominant chord that requires resolution on the tonic. Mozart's musical design appears to be mocking the two friends' shared adoration, or it could at least be interpreted in this way. This is what happened in the performance recorded by Sir John Eliot Gardiner for the DG label in 1993, in which the singers extended the last "tali" in such a way as to make the rapturous sentiment of the two friends look ridiculous and melodramatic.

The second trio, "È la fede delle femine," is the E major response to the recitative. Don Alfonso and the two friends continue to defend opposing

EXAMPLE 2. Bars 18–21, recitative "Fuor la spada," act 1, scene 1

positions, now with regard to the metaphor of the phoenix, an old literary cliché that Da Ponte borrowed from the librettist Pietro Metastasio.[12] Don Alfonso states that female fidelity is just like the phoenix, a bird that everyone claims exists but no one has ever seen. In their response to Don Alfonso, the doubles compete with each other for the first time: They sing the same phrases, alternately, both affirming that their beloved is the "Fenice." As the phoenix is unique, only one of the women can aspire to this position. In this way, an unconscious rivalry is established between them. In addition, towards the end of the number, Mozart begins to play with words in an amusing way. Via alternate singing of the verses, a typical device in ensemble numbers, he creates a new phrase by surprise whose meaning is unacceptable for the doubles, by adding fragments of Don Alfonso's part to that of the two friends. The complete text sung by Don Alfonso is "la fede delle femine . . . dove sia, nessun lo sa" (the fidelity of women . . . where it is, no one knows), while Guglielmo and Ferrando sing "La fenice è Fiordiligi" (The phoenix is Fiodiligi) and "La fenice è Dorabella" (The phoenix is Dorabella) respectively. However, between bars 45 and 51 (Example 3), the three men sing alternately, separating the different elements of their phrases, so that what we hear is "dove sia" "Fiordiligi," "dove sia" "Dorabella," "nessun lo sa" (where is Fiordiligi, where is Dorabella, nobody knows). The result is a musical joke in which no one knows where the two women are (and therefore what they are doing), which is exactly the opposite of what the two friends have been repeatedly insisting. It is as if Mozart were anticipating the infidelity that will

EXAMPLE 3. Bars 45–51, terzetto "È la fede delle femine," act 1, scene 1, no. 2

later take place. In addition, the four syllables of the words "nessun lo sa" are sung on separate forte notes, as if to announce a key principle, in a musical design that is highly reminiscent of the "Così fan tutte" motif.[13]

The scene ends with a second recitative and the last terzetto, "Una bella serenata," in which the men agree on the wager that will lead to all the unpleasant events that later unfold. The only remarkable thing from the point of view of mimetic desire occurs in the terzetto, in which for the first time we notice a slight difference in the character of the two friends: Ferrando appears more idealistic and exalted, singing with a high-flying melody of his dream to serenade his beloved, whereas Guglielmo, more pragmatic and down to earth with a melody of short phrases, suggests offering a banquet.[14] This difference, although subtle, may be related to the typification of the male roles in opera buffa, according to which Ferrando would fall into the group of highly regarded or heroic characters with a high tessitura, while Guglielmo belongs to the group of more ordinary, more vulgar characters of low tessitura. Thus in terms of tessitura, their perfect partners would be precisely the opposite of those they have chosen as lovers. In this way, at the beginning of the opera it is suggested, musically speaking, that the initial pairing is unnatural, contrary to convention, and therefore contrary to musical beauty and harmony. What is interesting is that these differences could be an obstacle to the perfect revelation of mimetic desire, in that Mozart might be tempted to depict in a more ideal, romantic, and spontaneous way the love or attraction between the protagonists whose voices are better matched, namely Ferrando and Fiordiligi on the one hand, and Guglielmo and Dorabella on the other. We will return to this issue later.

TABLE 8. Texts of the duet "Ah guarda sorella!" (act 1, scene 2, no. 4), according to singing types

		FIORDILIGI	DORABELLA
Andante	alternate singing	1. *Ah guarda, sorella! Se boca più bella, Se aspetto più nobile . . .* Ah, look, sister, if you can find a more beautiful mouth, a nobler aspect	2. *Osserva tu un poco, che foco ha ne'sguardi! Se fiamma, se dardi . . .* Observe you a little, the fire of his glance! If he does not seem to shoot flames, if he does not seem to shoot arrows
		3. *Sembiante guerriero, ed amante* One sees in his face a warrior and a lover	4. *Faccia che alletta e minaccia* One sees a face that seduces and that threatens
Transition	duet singing	5. *Felice son'io / Io sono felice* How happy I am / I am so happy!	
Allegro	duet singing	6. *Se questo mio core mai cangia desio, amore mi faccia vivendo penar* If ever my heart should change its desire, may love make me live in pain	

After the male doubles have been presented to the audience, it is now the turn of the women. In scene 2, which takes place in a small garden, a two-part duetto ("Ah guarda, sorella," no. 4, Andante-Allegro) is used to introduce the two sisters. The texture of the duetto, as is usual in such numbers, is governed by the parallelism of construction. Fiordiligi and Dorabella praise their respective objects of desire in identical fashion, singing alternately during the Andante before coming together in a duet for the final Allegro. The discourse is "rigorously identical,"[15] as can be seen in Table 8, which compares the texts sung by the two sisters.

Each woman parades the qualities of her lover before her sister's eyes: "guarda" (look), "osserva" (observe). At the very least, they are pushing each other towards imitation, something that is admirably expressed by both the

EXAMPLE 4. Bars 83–91, duetto "Ah guarda, sorella," act 1, scene 2, no. 4

text and the music, in that in the proposals made by each woman as they sing alternately, there are clear parallels between the textual and musical constructions. In addition, by praising their treasured possession, they are each stimulating the other's desire, albeit unconsciously. This alternating singing part of the Andante is followed by a brief transitional passage to the Allegro, in which both sisters sing an identical melodic phrase together, at a distance of a third, so expressing the identical happiness that is overwhelming them. Fiordiligi sings "Felice son'io" and Dorabella sings "Io sono felice." For Brown,[16] this is an example of exchange and imitation, an indication of envy between the sisters. However, it could also be understood as perfect communion and identification, because although the listener hears "son'io" and "felice" at the same time, they have no problem understanding their full meaning, mixed together by the music in a way that only it can achieve, thanks to the consonant intervals.

In the Allegro, the usual fast final section of a duet, the two women sing these reckless words together: "Se questo mio core mai cangia desio, amore mi faccia vivendo penar" (If ever my heart should change its desire, may love make me live in pain). These words are an unintentional foreshadowing of what is to come. They will indeed suffer, because the object of their desire will change. Mozart makes fun of their feelings of amorous excitement, by hinting to the listener that perhaps this is false. To all appearances, they are truly in love when they sing the word "amore" together twice (bars 83–91), the first time with a long note that ends in a graceful crotchet and the second with another long note that ends in a melisma in thirds. But while the long notes are sounding (Example 4), in the instrumental accompaniment we hear ascending scales on bassoon and cello, the first time on the tonic A, and the second on the dominant E. They are so flat and affirmative that they seem out of place in the midst of such apparent rapture. Suddenly the two women both seem ridiculous, even false, causing the listener to smile.

Brown detects "signs of envy" in the singing of the sisters, as each one "incorporates elements from the other's description."[17] He is referring to the interchange of the long note on the vowel "a" of "penar," which he claims could be part of an exchange between them about the fidelity of which each boasts. This claim could be open to question, but it is striking that Brown highlights examples of imitation of desire, even though he shows little interest in uncovering the intricacies of this theme in *Così fan tutte*.

We should note that, despite the obvious parallels in the singing that dominate the duet, and that express the identification between the doubles and a probable envious imitation, there are slight musical differences between the two, something we have already seen in the musical characterization of the male doubles. Fiordiligi is more solemn and delicate, her melody is more continuous, the instrumental accompaniment is light (bars 15ff.), and the qualities displayed in her beloved's face are those of a warrior and a lover ("guerriero ed amante"). Dorabella, however, is more playful and abrupt, her phrases are shorter, the instrumental accompaniment is much fuller and in staccato (bars 35ff.), and for her the face of her beloved is both charming and threatening ("alletta e minaccia").

This duet is related to the *duettino* "Al fato dàn legge" (scene 4, no. 7), the first performed by the two men. Although the *duettino* is often omitted in modern productions of the opera, as it is not particularly important from a musical point of view, it is nevertheless relevant to my theme. Sung at the time when the two friends claim to have been summoned away to the front, they homophonically express the same identical desire, which is to return to the arms of their lovers. It is a lying wish, because in fact they are not going to leave, but it is not necessarily feigned, because they really want everything to stay the same. The two sing together all the time and, in the final intensification, each in turn sings a broad melisma while the other holds a long note on the word "tornar." In this way, the music is showing us that the two friends are possessed by the same feeling of desire. However, it is a desire that they exchange, imitate, and copy from each other. Brown points out the similarity with the two sisters' duet previously discussed, in which they exchange the long note on the word "penar" near the end.[18] As much as I would like this to be true, it is clear, however, that this resort to imitation is also a typical feature of a duet, since long notes held by one of the duet partners while the other performs an embellishment or diminution is a commonplace in this genre.

In conclusion, I can affirm that at the beginning of the opera *Così fan tutte* there is a clear intention to show, through music and words, the extreme similarity between the characters of the same sex, to the point that they can be viewed as doubles. Musical and literary analysis has shown us that this identification of the doubles is deliberately evident, and that even in the music, there are small details highlighting how the characters copy and imitate each other when they sing in duet, all of which is lightly seasoned with touches of musical mockery. Just as the closeness of the doubles is a common device in literature that seeks to reveal the mechanisms of imitative desire, as Girard has shown, in *Così* the initial closeness between Ferrando and Guglielmo, and between Fiordiligi and Dorabella, is an essential condition for their subsequent rivalry. The subtle hints of difference between the doubles only serve to strengthen the suspicion of a latent rivalry. Let us recall that while throughout act 1 the two pairs remain united, the men in their vain attempts at seduction and the women in their rejection of these advances, in act 2 the two sisters, spurred on by Despina and by their suitors' persistent flattery, unblock this impasse by unleashing the rivalry between them, deciding to follow their hearts and surrender to their new lovers. At the same time, the two men each pursue the other's prized possession until at last they secure it. The result is that both pairs suffer jealousy, envy, and, inevitably, disappointment.[19]

Mechanisms of Desire

The Test as a Central Feature

The rising action phase of *Così fan tutte* is triggered by the acceptance of a wager on the outcome of an experiment or test, which becomes the central theme of the opera: If we tempt women with new lovers, will they be faithful to their old ones, or will they cast them aside? In other words, if we present a new object to someone and we present it to them as desirable, will they make it their desired object, or will they reject it? If they reject it, they will show firmness and loyalty to the previous object of their desire, but if they accept it, they will show weakness and betrayal. From a Girardian perspective, this is a false dilemma, because humans will inevitably accept this new desire and will not choose to reject it. When they do so, they will firmly believe that they have made their own original decision, that it has not been externally induced or imposed on them, but the fact is they will have followed the irrepressible human impulse to imitate or copy. Don Alfonso would agree with this theory. Indeed, he plays a fundamental role in the holding of the test: It is he who first broaches the subject while at the same time advising them not to go ahead with it, because he knows how it will end. The test is not a cruel experiment conceived by a cynical Don Alfonso, but a warning or lesson aimed at curing the two couples of their immaturity about love.[20] In this "school of lovers," the original title of the libretto that Mozart kept as a subtitle, the test is absolutely essential in order to uncover the truth about individual feelings. It is a way of putting the lovers through a "school" of physical desires, jealousy, shame, and grief, in the belief that this will educate their feelings. They cannot merely stand back and watch others undergo the test; they must do it themselves. Thus, the test is not "like a formal game that results in brutal disillusionment, and instead should be viewed as an essential stage for the progress of the heart and reason."[21]

The key role played by the test in *Così fan tutte* is evident, as happens in all the possible ancient sources of the libretto, from the tales of Cephalus and Procris, Collatinus and Tarquinius, and the various stories from *Orlando furioso* or Boccaccio's *Decameron*, to Cervantes's *El curioso impertinente* or Shakespeare's *Cymbeline*. In all these stories, the authors present situations in which preconceived ideals that ignore the reality of human feelings are doomed to fail. In Mozart and Da Ponte's time, testing the fidelity of women in love was a conventional theme of opera buffa, as Hunter reminds us.[22] This suggests that they wanted to highlight the weakness of female fidelity, at that time regarded as a social "defect" by rejecting it through mockery and laughter. But Mozart and Da Ponte turn that theme into a deeper reflection: It is not a fault, nor a weakness, but an inexorable human law.

Incitement, Envy, and Rivalry

It is part of human nature that we want what we don't have. As soon as we get something, we want something else—especially if it is presented to us as desirable by someone else, who acts as a mediator. This could be anyone. In the case of the male doubles in *Così fan tutte*, it is Don Alfonso who first plays the role of inciter-inducer, in much the same way as Ariosto's sorceress Melissa, by questioning the fidelity of their beloveds. The wise old philosopher role played by Don Alfonso is quite similar to that played by Pandarus in Shakespeare's *Troilus and Cressida*, whom Girard asserts is "the mediator of all mediators," the scheming instigator of mimetic reactions, whose "initial push sets entire worlds in motion."[23]

Don Alfonso knows that the soldiers are very proud and cannot bear to have their fiancées' honor called into question. He also knows perfectly well that by claiming their sweethearts would be unfaithful to them if they were put to the test, he is planting a seed, an idea that would otherwise never have occurred to them. He is stimulating a desire to obtain something they do not have, the certainty of their fidelity, or even more: the human desire for another person to confirm, by displaying their desire for it, that what we possess is desirable. Despite Don Alfonso's claims that it would be better not to do the test, merely by mentioning the possibility he has done enough to make the two friends determined to do it. They will be incapable of restraining their "pazzo desire." In fact, what he does is incite their desire to possess the women again. He also encourages rivalry between them, since the only way to obtain certainty is by arousing the other's desire. As Girard states in his analysis of Dostoevsky's *The Eternal Husband*: "If Pavel Pavlovitch tries madly to get Veltchaninov interested in his fiancée, it is not because he wants him to win her heart but because he wants him to desire her, so confirming and to some extent endorsing Pavel's decision to choose her." "The rival,"

Girard continues, "is the only person with authority in the matter of desire; he alone can confer on the object the stamp of the infinitely desirable by desiring that object himself."[24]

Consequently, the only way of performing the test is by inciting the other to desire what we possess. The other's desire confirms our possession and rekindles our own desire, which had been extinguished once you obtained possession. In this way, another mediator arises: the friend, the double, the rival. In *Così*, both boys apparently want the other to fail, that is, to not win their beloved's heart. But deep down what they want is to put their possession in jeopardy, by putting it within reach of the other as a means of reviving their own desire for it. It is a very risky business, a "crazy desire," with potentially catastrophic, predictable consequences. Musically, this whole process is established by the doubles in the first scene, and throughout act 1 it is reaffirmed in the repeated attempts at seduction.

However, the desire and the rivalry between the male doubles reach a much more critical point late in act 2, when, after Guglielmo has succeeded in snatching Ferrando's sweetheart in the duetto of scene 5 (no. 23, "Il core vi donno"), the two men meet to report on their progress as seducers. Ferrando is unaware of Dorabella's betrayal, and the audience is expectantly awaiting his reaction when he first finds out. Mozart and Da Ponte devote two complete scenes, 8 and 9, to this moment. These scenes consist of a sequence made up of two recitatives (secco and *accompagnato*), an aria by Guglielmo, a new *accompagnato* recitative, and a cavatina by Ferrando. This enables the action to be played out more slowly over this planned sequence, so as to allow the audience to carefully observe the changes in Ferrando's mood and desire. The whole process begins with a secco recitative between Guglielmo and Ferrando, "Amico, abbiamo vinto!" (Friend, we have won!). The latter explains to his friend in detail how he has tried to seduce Fiordiligi, how he has spoken tenderly to her, deploying all the necessary strategies of seduction . . . only to fail. The two friends embrace. It is now Guglielmo's turn, who, after some hesitation, ends up confessing to Ferrando that Dorabella has surrendered to his charms. At that moment, the secco recitative becomes *accompagnato*, a musical style used in opera to express agitated, confused thought. The strings play brief motifs to underline Ferrando's mixed feelings, which oscillate between anger ("Ah perfida!"—Ah, wicked one! bars 64–65), sadness ("Numi! Tante promesse"—Gods! So many promises, bars 78ff.), and

EXAMPLE 5. Bars 8–15, Overture

despair ("Che fare or deggio?"—What should I do now? bars 83ff.). Finally, he appeals to his friend for advice, who then closes the scene with an aria criticizing women, (no. 26 "Donne mie" Women of mine), a cliché feature of eighteenth-century opera buffa.

The following scene (9), which features Ferrando almost exclusively, is of more interest for the subject we are discussing. He is alone and, once again using the style of the *accompagnato* recitative, he declares his confusion, his "disordine di pensieri" (disorder of thoughts), and plots revenge against Dorabella. However, just as he sings, in a tragic C minor, the word "cancellarla" (erase her, referring to Dorabella), the music changes to an Andante in E-flat major, the relative major of the key he has been using up until then. The sudden change of both key and mode is a sign that Ferrando's feelings are also beginning to change, and he soon acknowledges that his heart still yearns for Dorabella. But this apparent mood swing lasts for barely a few bars, as Ferrando immediately begins a cavatina, a brief two-part aria in which he expresses these contradictions (no. 27, "Tradito, schernito"). The text of the aria is also divided into two parts, like Ferrando's feelings. The first part is an angry outburst ("Tradito, schernito"—Betrayed, mocked) in C minor, which unfolds in a seven-bar broken phrase that ascends from piano to forte, until it is finally left hanging on the dominant of the key. A general pause follows before, suddenly, the clarinets and bassoons propose a new theme in E-flat major, indicated in the score as "dolce." This gives way to the second

EXAMPLE 6. Bars 20–26, Andante "Tutti acusan le donne," act 2, scene 13, no. 30

part of the text, in which Ferrando admits that he still loves Dorabella. The whole text is repeated from bar 30 onwards, and in the final intensification, it becomes clear that of the two conflicting feelings with which Ferrando is wrestling, love is the one that prevails. In other words, and somewhat incomprehensibly, the pain of betrayal has made his love stronger. Desire has been reborn in him immediately after he realizes that his rival now possesses the object that once belonged to him. His newfound desire for Dorabella springs precisely from the fact that she now belongs to Guglielmo. In case we were in any doubt, in the recitative that brings scene 9 to a close, once Guglielmo and Don Alfonso have returned, a vain Guglielmo boasts to his friend that he is better than him, "di più merto" (more deserving), thus throwing down a new gauntlet and sparking in Ferrando the desire to imitate him. As we know, Ferrando soon succeeds in seducing Fiordiligi, in the duet "Fra gli amplessi" (scene 12, no. 29). This is followed by a recitative in which Ferrando revels in his success, ironically asking Guglielmo who is "de più merto" now.

At this stage, the two friends are now deeply immersed in their rivalry contest, which seems likely to continue escalating, gathering seemingly unstoppable momentum. Fortunately, however, Don Alfonso intervenes in scene 13, announcing first in secco recitative and then in an Andante, (no. 30, "Tutti acusan le donne"—Everyone blames women) the fundamental principle that he has defended all along: The fickleness of our desires is part of human nature, and there can be no exceptions; it is a "necessità del core" (need of the heart). Don Alfonso summarizes the situation and the moral of the story in a royal octave, a serious form that, in comedy, is used to indicate an important moment in the story has been reached.[25] Mozart's music collaborates by highlighting this passage. Among other things, when the men intone the words "Così fan tutte," the motto from the Overture can be heard again and in the same key, C major, which according to Steptoe[26] is the key of the opera and the key Mozart uses when he wants to present reality exactly as it is (see Examples 5 and 6).

Turning to the female doubles: They too are incited to desire, and to a greater extent than the men, in that not only do all the characters conspire to seduce them, but all the rivalry between them is made clear from the very beginning, as mentioned earlier in the duet "Ah, guarda sorella." To facilitate the analysis, I will now study the question of female doubles around two central themes: on the one hand, the moments of incitement of desire, of inducement to passion, involving all the various inciters (all the characters except for Fiordiligi); and on the other hand, the moments in which the two sisters reject desire. This rejection is so exaggerated that it seems feigned and false, so revealing the opposite of what it is apparently trying to show.

The desire for the new lovers that gradually grows within Fiordiligi and Dorabella is not the product of love at first sight. The passion they feel is not spontaneous but induced: The possibility of desiring someone else is suggested to them by Despina, by Don Alfonso, and by the disguised Ferrando and Guglielmo. Even Fiordiligi's ultimate surrender to desire is itself induced by Dorabella's desire. Induced passion is one of the themes to which Girard returns again and again, for example in his analysis of the story of Paolo and Francesca, the lovers in Dante's *Divine Comedy*.[27] Paolo and Francesca do not fall romantically in love, and instead are drawn to each other by imitation of the model, which in their case is the book that they are reading together about the love shared by Lancelot and Guinevere: "The book, the model, is present from the beginning; it is the model that originates their future self-absorption." Girard adds incisively, "It is the book itself, Francesca maintains, that plays the role of diabolical go-between . . . it has to be some person's word that suggests desire."[28] In *Così*, this role is first played by the maid, Despina.

There are two moments in the opera when Despina intervenes to encourage the two sisters to surrender to passion: in the recitative and the aria (no. 12) that closes scene 9 of act 1, and in the aria (no. 19) that opens act 2. In these numbers the interest lies more in the words than in the music, which does little more than highlight the clichés typical of the maid-confidante character in opera buffa. My analysis will therefore focus on the libretto, without referring to the music. In the first of her two interventions, Despina enters her mistresses' room and finds the two women dejected after bidding farewell to their lovers. To cheer them up, she suggests that there are many other men that they could meet ("vi restan tutti gli altri"—all the others are left), so sowing the seeds of their desire to possess something they do not have. To overcome their scruples, she intones "In uomini, in soldati" (no. 12), an aria deprecating men for their numerous failings, the reverse of the one sung later by Guglielmo (no. 26). In the aria, Despina claims that fidelity cannot be expected from men, as they belong to a "razza indiscreta" (indiscreet race[29]), and warns the sisters that their lovers will stop desiring them as soon as they have possessed them ("Poi ci dispregiano"—At once they despise us). Finally, she proposes that they should love men purely for the purposes of convenience or vanity but without remorse. In fact, she is warning them of a great truth: namely that desire, even their own desire, will die once the object has been possessed. But it will be to no avail. The important thing is that, through her mediation, both sisters begin to feel tempted to look for a new object of desire, even before the two "Albanians" first appear.

Despina's second contribution, at the beginning of act 2, takes place in a very different atmosphere. The two sisters have just divided up their new lovers between them (who gets who), and the ground is now fertile for Despina to plant her seed with her aria "Una donna a quindici anni" (no. 19). As in the previous aria, she describes a stereotyped figure, that of the flirtatious woman who proficiently wields the weapons of seduction. This role model is held up before the two sisters, who are attracted by it. What Despina is doing is to pique their curiosity and their vanity, and to show them how to satisfy both without feeling remorse. They convince themselves that they are in love again, and, at the same time, that they want to remain faithful to

EXAMPLE 7. Bars 39–42, recitative "Che sussurro!" act 1, scene 11

their fiancés. In other words, the women believe that they have resisted while what they really want is to fall, because of the desire they have felt, from the very first moment, for the new objects that have been placed before them. They reject their suitors' advances while in fact wishing to be seduced. In this way, they fit the description of the Marivaudian coquette analyzed by Girard in his article "Marivaudage and Hypocrisy." Fiordiligi and Dorabella resemble Marivaux's coquettes, who enjoy feeling desired while believing "they are innocent and respectable."[30] At heart, Fiordiligi and Dorabella are hypocrites, not liars. And in addition to being coquettes, they are also Tartuffes: Marivaux's archetype of Tartuffe "is a man who plays his role so well that he confuses it with his own nature and manages to convince himself that he is genuinely religious."[31]

Together with Despina, Ferrando and Guglielmo also play a fundamental role in the game of incitement to desire, as we might expect. There are at least three such occasions in act 1 alone. The first takes place in the *accompagnato* recitative in scene 11, during the passage featuring the two men, now disguised as foreigners (bars 26ff.). Their first attempt at conquest is brilliantly designed by Mozart. Both the melodies in a minor key and the string accompaniment in long notes come together to create a great irresistible beauty, an apparent sincerity in their amorous feelings. The women cannot help being attracted, and nor can we. Guglielmo and Ferrando sing alternately, each completing the other's phrases, as if they were one voice, one person. In reality the two friends are improvising and lying, as they lengthen each phrase with metaphors, each more clichéd than the last but with marvelously beautiful, moving music. In the last lines, "per implorar pietade / in flebil metro" (to implore pity / in plaintive tones), they end up acknowledging that they are to be pitied (Example 7). This could be understood as a stereotypical lament, but Mozart seems to want to cast it in an ironic light, as for the final line he designs a separate musical conclusion, a short descending motive (bars 41–42) that is quite simple, at least when compared to the fiery duet we have just heard and, above all, compared to the very passionate measure that the two men have just performed together, in C minor and with a long sustained note on the word "pietade."

In this musical joke, Mozart is suggesting that the two men are very bad at producing original, artistic lines, and by extension Da Ponte is too, although such an absurd claim could only provoke laughter from the audience. In short, in this recitative, the music is telling us that the men's seduction strategies are being parodied. It is important that these strategies are properly presented. They have to be applied so that the two women can succumb to them. And if this were a serious opera rather than a buffa, there would be no parody at all.[32] In this case, however, as spectators of a comic opera, we understand not only the seduction but also the highlighting and the criticism of the hypocrisy that lies behind the men's attempts to conquer the two women. We are delighted when the lie is revealed.

The next person to arouse desire in others is Guglielmo, also in scene 11 of act 1, in no. 15, "Nos siate ritrosi." We are now very close to the finale, and things do not seem to be going as Don Alfonso had predicted, since the two girls appear adamant in their rejection of their new suitors. In fact, Fiordiligi has just sung the aria "Come scoglio," in which she has stated that, far from giving in, she will stand firm as a rock. Guglielmo decides to reply to such a sublime intention with a lighthearted aria in which he flaunts their physical qualities as men before the women's eyes. He makes a flattering description of himself and his friend: "Siam forti e ben fatti . . . Abbiamo bel piede, / bell'occhio, bel naso . . . E questi mustacchi / chiamare si possono / trionfi degli uomini" (We are strong and well-built . . . We have beautiful

EXAMPLE 8. Bars 44–52, Guglielmo's aria "Non siate ritrosi," act 1, scene 11, no. 15

feet / beautiful eyes, beautiful nose . . . And these mustaches / can be called / the triumphs of men). He then invites the women to look at, observe, and touch them ("guardate," "osservate," "toccate"). Such a qualitative leap, this clear allusion to the most physical side of love, scandalizes the two girls, who storm off. Musically, the piece is simple but interesting: It is arranged to provoke their desire to look, observe, and touch. For example, between bars 45 and 52 (Example 8), Guglielmo sings the following lines: "Guardate bel piede, osservate bell'occhio, toccate bel naso, il tutto osservate" (Look at the beautiful foot, observe the beautiful eye, touch the beautiful nose, observe the whole). The verbs and physical elements of the description are sung individually, separated by silences, and the melody ascends through the notes of the dominant chord, whose harmony governs the whole passage, which for the time being is left unresolved, in suspension. In addition, in the instrumental part, Guglielmo's singing is accompanied by woodwind and strings, alternating two motifs (one dotted and the other in very brief values, almost like an ornament) as they ascend with him through the chord. All this produces tension and urgency, an irresistible invitation to give in to temptation.

In this aria by Guglielmo, there is one more aspect worth highlighting. It is about vanity as a prerequisite for the excitement of desire, a theme discussed by Girard in his analysis of Marivaux's comedies: "In Marivaux's battle of the sexes, the two partners succeed in impressing each other insofar as they manage to be impressed with themselves."[33] In other words, the admiration that Guglielmo and Ferrando profess for themselves has a purpose, namely, to excite the women's admiration, to arouse their desire. It is also important to remember that it was vanity that led the two men to accept the wager,[34] and of course, the flattered vanity of Fiordiligi and Dorabella will help push both of the women towards attaining their desires.

A qualitative leap in the induction of desire takes place in the finale of act 1, in which the situation becomes increasingly tense until the two women's resistance is finally worn down, albeit only momentarily. In the opera buffa genre, the finale always follows certain conventions, both dramatic and musical. In musical terms, the normal alternation of recitatives, arias, and ensemble numbers is replaced in the finale by an unbroken chain of musical numbers. There is no letup in the music as it advances inexorably towards the final Presto. Another convention is to add voices to the ensemble as the characters arrive on stage, in this case advancing from a duo to a sextet. At the same time, there are a whole array of unexpected plot twists and turns that resolve certain situations and complicate others. Dramatic tension and musical tension increase, reinforcing each other.

The finale of act 1 starts with a duet by Fiordiligi and Dorabella ("Ah che tutta in un momento," scene 14, no. 18), who together mourn their fiancés' absence. The words we hear are supposed to suggest that, for them, nothing has changed since the men left for the war. However, the music hints at

EXAMPLE 9. Bars 32–38, finale, act 1, scene 14

something that neither woman dares to declare, that deep down inside them nests a certain frivolity, a coquetry that they cannot publicly express but are beginning to feel. This is clearly heard in the graceful dialogue between the flute and the bassoon, which is twice inserted into the discourse between the two women, interrupting the languid flow of the strings: the first time in the instrumental prelude (bars 6–9), and the second time immediately after singing the first stanza, as an accompaniment to the beginning of the second (bars 32–38, Example 9). This engenders doubt and suspicion in the mind of the listeners.

Without giving us a moment to think about this, the music then launches us into the next number (scene 15). The two "Albanians" rush in, followed by Don Alfonso, and pretend to poison themselves, apparently in despair after their advances have been spurned. Despina and Don Alfonso actively collaborate in encouraging the two girls to approach the men to try to console them. The sisters want to rush to their sides, but they resist because of their promises to their fiancés. At the same time, however, it would be wrong to refuse charity and sympathy to dying men, and with this excuse they finally approach them. In this way the road to passion is smoothed by compassion. Fiordiligi and Dorabella are given a way of consenting to desire for acceptable reasons. By this ruse, desire is hypocritically disguised as compassion, so as not to appear so obvious. Mozart writes this scene in G minor, a tragic key. The verses, and especially the verse endings, abound in words in which the stress falls on the third-to-last syllable (sdrucciolo line endings), which is traditionally reserved for tragic scenes: "orribili," "lasciatemi," "arsenico" "liberi," "tragico," "espettacolo," "barbare," "avvicinatevi," "anima" (horrible, leave me, arsenic, free, tragic, spectacle, barbarous, come closer, soul). In the last part of this section in G minor (bars 117ff.), the singing of the words is cut off by silences, so that everyone sings in a broken voice to denote that they can hardly speak—the men because they are dying, the women because they are horrified, and Don Alfonso because he is collaborating in the deceit. Despina, who has rushed in in response to her ladies' cries for help, encourages them to comfort the dying, before leaving with Don Alfonso to look for a doctor. This prompts Mozart to write a quartet between the four lovers and to prepare the first break in the women's resistance. The key is now E-flat major. In the first few bars (198–218), the two pairs convey their feelings separately; the women express horror while the men, feigning dying, offer mocking asides. In bar 219 the music starts to change, through a minor mode motive of the first violins, which breaks out alone in an ascending and descending pattern, in much the same way as a person taking a deep breath (Example 10). This is followed immediately by a brief interjection from Ferrando and Guglielmo, which is replicated again by the violin motive. Fiordiligi and Dorabella notice the deep sighs of the "infelici" (poor wretches) (bars 224–226) and confer between themselves, convincing each other that they should approach. All this happens in a few bars, in which the first and second violins are constantly exchanging the lamenting motive. The music suggests and accompanies, cleverly insinuating that Fiordiligi and Dorabella's firm stance is being undermined and that their desire is being revealed. They approach, take the men's hands, touch their foreheads, and Dorabella even

EXAMPLE 10. Bars 218–222, finale, act 1, scene 15

goes so far as to frivolously comment "Che figure interessanti!" (What interesting creatures!).

Immediately after this number, in scene 16, Despina appears disguised as a doctor, accompanied by Don Alfonso, and cures the two "dying" men with a session of mesmerism. This particular scene in the finale of act 1 not only appeals to the women's sense of pity but also highlights how physical contact can spread desire, making clear sexual allusions. According to Moindrot,[35] at that time mesmerism was practiced mainly on women, who were aroused by the experiment. *Così*'s audience must have understood the sexual connotations, especially when in this scene "the characters touch each other for the first time." As if that were not enough, the physical contagion of desire is confirmed and reinforced by the music, which in an opera finale always involves a breakneck escalation: The characters lose their singularity, become confused and equal, and can "freely express their contradictory feelings."[36] We could also consider, according to Pierpaolo Polzonetti's interpretation,[37] that the fake poison causes a "contagion," an infectious lovesickness that has spread to both couples, and that the mesmeric cure only makes it worse. In this way, the four lovers are left defenseless, completely exposed to their own desires, incapable of controlling the situation. This point of view is enormously useful for my purposes, partly because of the terms that Polzonetti uses and partly because of his observations about desire. In his analysis, for example, he uses the term "contagious disease" in relation to the awakening of desire and depicts the poison as a form of "love potion" that can change the direction of desire. This is reminiscent of Girard's interpretation of the magical love potion made from a flower called "love-in-idleness" and used by Shakespeare in his comedy *A Midsummer Night's Dream*.[38] Polzonetti also refers to the two men's loss of control over their own feelings as the infection spreads and even goes so far as to speculate about Fiordiligi's unconscious desire for her foreign lover. However, his ideas are still somewhat removed from those of mimetic theory in that, among other things, he gives a Freudian interpretation of Fiordiligi's unconscious and claims that the fidelity test did not have the outcome the two friends were hoping for, when according to a more Girardian interpretation, they obtained exactly what they were looking for, albeit unconsciously. In fact, each man desires not only the other's partner, but also that their partner be seduced by their rival, so as to stoke their own desire even more strongly.

In the midst of this paroxysm, however, the men suddenly ruin the intricate seduction process by blatantly asking for a kiss (Allegro, bars 485ff.). Their request is rejected out of hand by the women, and act 1 ends with a loud din and plenty of movement, in terms of both the music and the on-stage action. The experiment has so far proved unsuccessful.

The Outburst of Desire

A large part of act 2 (scenes 4 to 12) is taken up by the preparation and development of the final conquest of the two sisters. As Kunze states, it is "the last joint attempt by the two disguised lovers to approach the girls."[39] This is where the ambiguities are to be resolved, when at last the two sisters openly choose to secure possession of their new object of desire. It all begins with a musical dinner in the garden (scene 4), which the "Albanians" have prepared in a new bid to conquer the girls. Despina and Don Alfonso encourage the lovers to sit together, before exiting the stage and leaving them alone. Doubts, embarrassment, shyness . . . no one dares to be the first to speak, until they start engaging in polite conversation in recitativo secco (scene 5). There are many unspoken desires, which are hard for them to make public. Finally, Fiordiligi and Ferrando get up to go for a walk. Guglielmo feels jealous but

EXAMPLE 11. Bars 12–16, recitative "Barbara! Perchè fuggi?" act 2, scene 6

soon decides to continue trying to win over Dorabella. The ensuing recitative between the two is an escalating dialogue, a battle of attacks and defenses, that becomes increasingly intense, until Dorabella finally capitulates with a simple "L'accetto" (I accept). This is immediately followed by a duet, which, like Dorabella's surrender, is simple and quick.[40] Their declaration of love is credible and sincere, even though the couple is "fake."

What has happened in the meantime with Ferrando and Fiordiligi? In scene 6, they are returning from their stroll, and both seem quite upset, especially Fiordiligi, who firmly rejects Ferrando. We hear an *accompagnato* recitative in G minor, the style used to show agitated, shifting feelings. Although the string section's aggressive remarks confirm Fiordiligi's sincerity, even dignity, in resisting, from bar 13 onwards the music also begins to warn us that something is about to change. The score is marked "Adagio," and the strings, departing from the motif with which they have been underlining Fiordiligi's rebuttal of her suitor's advances, then move on to a delicate motif that is repeated four times, alternating with the lines of dialogue between the two. The motif prompts Fiordiligi to intone "Tu vuoi tormi la pace" (You want to steal my peace), a complaint that is echoed by Ferrando with an almost identical melody and the words "Me per farti felice" (But to make you happy) (Example 11). The two phrases complement each other musically, because they are antecedent and consequent, question and answer.

The union of the two musical phrases reveals that the mutual feelings are not as divergent as we might suppose from the text they are singing. For the audience, it is clear that Fiordiligi is close to surrendering to her desire. But suddenly, after a minor mode recitative intended as a tragic, sensitive moment, Mozart returns us to the comedy for the last three bars. Ferrando asks Fiordiligi, before leaving her alone, to regale him with a glance. The violins echo this request with an insinuating, amusing motif, leaving us in suspense as to whether she may perhaps look over at him as he leaves (Example 12).

EXAMPLE 12. Bars 18–23, recitative "Barbara! Perchè fuggi?" act 2, scene 6

As we can see, the ambiguity between honesty and falsehood, truth and lies, is a constant feature of this opera. There can be no doubt that the music is leading us from one extreme to the other. Mozart plays with us, or rather guides us, through the twists and turns of the characters' psychology by means of music rather than through words or actions.

Once Fiordiligi has been left alone, she returns to the *accompagnato* recitative style. There is no trace of falsity or ambiguity in the music, and it could hardly be called parody. Fiordiligi feels guilty about her love for Ferrando and struggles with remorse. The recitative leads into an aria-rondo (no. 25, "Per pietà ben mio"), in which Fiordiligi inwardly apologizes to her fiancé

EXAMPLE 13. Bars 30–33, aria-rondo "Per pietà," act 2, scene 7, no. 25

for almost betraying him and promises to remain true. She sings a beautiful, heartfelt aria, in which she expresses apparently genuine, unfeigned love. For Patricia Lewy, for example, this rondo marks the climax of the opera, the moment when the music reveals that the character is moving from parody to sincerity.[41] For Michel Noiray it is the opera's most important aria, and its introductory Adagio "reveals a particularly deep and painful introspection" on the part of Fiordiligi.[42] However, in this number there is an unusual musical detail, the accompaniment of the horns, that is difficult to interpret because its function is not clear. Here the horns have an exceptional, almost soloistic role, especially at two particular points: the "sempre ascoso" fermata (bars 7–9 and 32–33, Example 13) and the "caro bene" long note (bars 46–48, Example 14, and 76–78) These horn motifs sound strange amidst the sensitivity of Fiordiligi's lament.

So, how should we interpret the role played by the horns here? What was Mozart trying to achieve? Is he again seeking to contradict the seriousness of a music he himself has so exquisitely prepared? Noiray offers us two

EXAMPLE 14. Bars 46–50, aria-rondo "Per pietà," act 2, scene 7, no. 25

possible explanations for the prominence of the horns in this aria: first, in the French comic opera tradition they represent "the voice of the absent loved one"; and second, they also represent the "horns" that were said to appear on a cuckold's head.[43] For his part, Brown interprets the horns as symbols of adultery that belie Fiordiligi's expressed intention to keep her desires secret and remain true to her fiancé.[44] Goehring agrees that from a musical point of view, the discourse offered by the horn passages is incongruent with what Fiordiligi is saying and with the feelings she is expressing.[45] He also asserts that the horns are like the voice of an onlooker who is commenting on the scene, such that Fiordiligi is not as alone as she might first have appeared. As happened in the previous number, "Come scoglio," in which the fact that the other characters are looking on leads the audience to think that Fiordiligi is being unwittingly insincere, in "Per pietà" she is also being observed and criticized, albeit by the music, something that the spectators pick up on.

Which of these interpretations should we choose? Once again, Mozart seems to be deliberately introducing a moment of ambivalence, the suspicion of a lie, as he does in so many of the numbers in this opera. If Mozart were truly determined to unveil the truth of the mechanisms of desire, crudely revealing how the characters deceive themselves as to their true motivations, as he has been doing up to this point in the opera, we would undoubtedly lean towards the second interpretation. However, in view of how the next stage in the drama is reflected in the music, I would prefer not to rule out the first option, namely that the horns are in fact invoking the figure of the absent beloved. Perhaps Mozart succumbed to the temptation to present Fiordiligi as genuinely, sincerely contrite, momentarily betraying the novelistic truth in favor of the romantic lie. This is not the last time such a doubt emerges, as a similar ambiguity appears a few moments later, in the scene in which Fiordiligi finally yields (scene 12).

Clearly it takes longer for Fiordiligi to surrender to the charms of her seducer than it does for Dorabella. Fiordiligi has a strong character, and to overcome her resistance a more profound, more insistent incitement to desire is required. The sterile struggle between prejudices, self-deception, and the inexorable law of human desires is played out and dragged out before us. Leaving the garden where Dorabella has just surrendered to Guglielmo and where Fiordiligi was torn between desire and guilt, we now find ourselves in a room where the three female protagonists, singing in recitativo secco, share their confidences. Fiordiligi finally acknowledges that she is in love with another man, although she continues to claim that she does not want to deceive Guglielmo. In an aria (no. 28, "È amore un ladroncello"—Love is a thief), Dorabella tries to convince Fiordiligi to yield, as she has done. The theme of this aria, that love is impossible to resist, was such a common feature of eighteenth-century opera buffa as to be expected by the audience. Raffaele Mellace, for example, has found similarities between the lines of this aria and those of the libretto of *Il Vecchio geloso* (The Jealous Old Man, Vienna 1767), an opera by Felice Alessandri and Baldassare Galuppi.[46] In an attempt to justify what she has done, Dorabella presents this buffa cliché of irresistible love and, in so doing, explains why "all women are like that." They have no choice. It is inevitable; it is impossible to resist love/desire. In this way, she is unwittingly confirming what Don Alfonso has been asserting since the beginning of the opera and also what Despina made clear in her two solo numbers.

After the aria, Dorabella and Despina depart the stage, leaving Fiordiligi alone (scene 11). The last we heard from her, in addition to a brief confession of her desire for "another," was sincere regret. We wonder if her sentiments have changed and to what extent her sister's readiness to express her feelings

TABLE 9. Structure of the duet "Fra gli amplessi," (act 2, scene 12, no. 29)

ADAGIO	CON PIÙ MOTO		ALLEGRO				LARGHETTO	ANDANTE
Bars 1–10	11–15	15–23	24–52	53–64	65–75		76–100	101–142
A	E	e →	C	→ d	D	→ a/A	A	A
			"Son tradita!"	"Incomincia a vacilar"	"Il tuo cor, o la mia morte"	"Ah, non son più forte" "Cedi, cara"	"Hai vinto" "Fa' di me quel che ti par"	
FL alone	FL alone	+ FD	FD + FL in alternate sung dialogue					FD + FL in duo

has left its mark on her. The doubts are immediately dispelled when, singing in recitativo secco, Fiordiligi affirms that she would rather die than fall and decides to leave in search of her fiancé on the battlefield. All signs of comedy have disappeared. Fiordiligi takes action, donning the uniform of . . . Ferrando! A preference unintentionally revealed? We might expect, perhaps, that at this point the music would provide an ironic or mocking comment on this situation. However, the number that begins as soon as the recitative has finished (no. 29, "Fra gli amplessi") defies all expectations, taking a completely unforeseen course. First of all, what starts as an apparently predictable aria in two parts, "Adagio"/"Con più moto," soon develops into a duet, with Ferrando's sudden appearance on stage. Thus, if we had any expectations regarding Fiordiligi's intentions to stand firm, as confirmed by the aria she has just begun to sing, we soon learn that these should be discarded, as the musical discourse offers no clues in this direction. Table 9 offers a detailed picture of the duet, helping us to trace the changes that take place and how the music and text combine in such effective ways.[47]

As the Adagio begins, Fiordiligi is enjoying imagining the moment when she and her fiancé are finally reunited. From the initial A major, she moves naturally to the key of the dominant, E major, in the liveliest section ("Con più moto"). However, just as her phrase is coming to an end on the cadenza on the tonic major chord, Ferrando appears. He replies to

EXAMPLE 15. Bars 11–21, duetto "Fra gli amplessi," act 2, scene 12, no. 29

Fiordiligi's phrase with no break in continuity, although the mode changes to E minor (Example 15). As Noiray makes clear, "Ferrando's intervention, just after the E cadenza, is extraordinarily effective, insofar as it combines the contradictory qualities of a continuation and an interruption."[48] There is indeed continuity with respect to the meter, as we are within the same stanza, so that the transition from Fiordiligi to Ferrando occurs naturally; there is also continuity in the melodic design, which the audience accepts as a complement to the question-answer format. Finally, continuity can also be seen in the tonality of E. By contrast, there is a clear break in the unexpected shift to the minor mode.

Fiordiligi's self-confidence is shattered, the inner turmoil produced by her desires returns, and with two exclamations in recitative style, "Cosa veggio!" and "Son tradita!" (What do I see! I have been betrayed!), she rushes into the Allegro in C Major. During this Allegro section, Ferrando and Fiordiligi sing alternately in a dialogue or exchange of phrases, which is increasingly urgent on Ferrando's part, increasingly pleading on Fiordiligi's. In the meantime, Mozart unites the two characters for a few bars, as they sing together that her fidelity "Incomincia a vacilar" (Is starting to waver). Of course, their doubts are working in opposite directions, in that if Fiordiligi were to waver, it would assuage all Ferrando's fears. In the music, this moment is highlighted by the introduction of several odd notes that do not belong to the scale of C major. This insinuates a modulation to D minor and, in so doing, helps create a sense of doubt or hesitation in the listener. The key of D minor is settled by a perfect cadence at the moment when Ferrando presents Fiordiligi with an impossible dilemma: "Il tuo cor, o la mia morte" (Your

EXAMPLE 16. Bars 91–96, duetto "Fra gli amplessi," act 2, scene 12, no. 29

heart or my death). Fiordiligi replies, like Zerlina in Don Giovanni's famous seduction duet, "Ah, non son più forte" (Ah, my strength is waning), and Ferrando insists up to four times with a "cedi, cara" (give in, my dear). This is accompanied by a new modulation, this time towards A minor, which soon reaches a cadence on the dominant chord, E major. We are about to return to A major, the key in which Fiordiligi began to sing, and Ferrando makes the most of his opportunity. In ternary tempo, "Larghetto," in a clear A major and with string accompaniment, he launches his final attack (Example 16) in just four verses, in which he offers himself as "sposo, amante, e più se vuoi" (husband, lover, or more if you want). Fiordiligi responds by asking God for guidance and issuing a final cry, "Crudel!" (Cruel!), which she sings in crescendo to forte only to be cut short in a sudden silence. Mozart then returns to the dynamic piano, makes the oboe sing a sweet melody, and at last, as if in whispers, we hear Fiordiligi's words of surrender: "Hai vinto. Fa' di me quel che ti par" (You have conquered. Do with me what you please). The last part of the duet, still in A major, restores the peace between the two lovers.

Ferrando and Fiordiligi now sing together until the end, united by the same words, which this time have an identical meaning for both of them.

As we can see, the musical discourse that Mozart has designed for this duet aims to highlight, subtly but clearly, the psychological changes that Fiordiligi is undergoing, from her initial determination to her final downfall. The most striking thing about this design is that it does not follow the conventions of opera buffa. In her analysis of the clichés of the buffo genre regarding noble characters such as Fiordiligi, Hunter points out how emotional conflict "tends to occur between rather than within individuals."[49] In other words, the characters' internal struggles are not revealed and do not usually lead to radical conversions or changes in principles. However, in Fiordiligi there is a conversion, and a very arduous one, full of remorse, regret, and resistance, which shows that, in this part of the opera at least, this character is treated seriously and is not part of the buffo. There is no parody in Fiordiligi in this duet, just truth. Moreover, Ferrando, the suitor, also ends up expressing genuine passion, and in A major, the only way to convince Fiordiligi, who, according to Steptoe, "is lost from the moment Ferrando touches A major."[50]

Most researchers who have analyzed this duet have reached similar conclusions, namely that it has no comic elements or that the music, at least, is serious and is not trying to parody the characters. Kunze, for example, states that the music suggests Mozart wants "to save an exceptional opportunity for happiness, in the conviction that love is an absolute right when it drives two noble beings whom everything brings closer together."[51] The same question arises again: Is Mozart breaching his general intention throughout the opera to reveal the mechanisms of desire, by allowing Fiordiligi to express feelings of romantic love, just as he did before in the rondo "Per pietà"? Is it possible to conclude, as Brèque does, that "with Ferrando, Mozart in fact betrays the meaning of the libretto"[52] by slipping back into the romantic lie? In my opinion, the naturalness and beauty displayed by the pairing of the two voices is so evident in this duet that it must have been a premeditated decision on the part of the composer. Mozart is simply fulfilling the expectations of an audience who never tire of the typical romantic scene when the two lovers finally come together in an idealized love duet, as played out again and again in opera and theater. He is also letting his characters enjoy, albeit fleetingly, the mirage of absolute love. However, a few scenes later, the sham will be revealed and, as a result, all the seriousness of the music of this duet will be revealed as false a posteriori.

Hypocrisy and *Méconnaissance*

Together with this ambiguity between the real and the false, the truth and the lie, there is another recurring feature in *Così* that is important to highlight, namely the overt intention to reveal hypocrisy and bring it center stage. Beneath the extreme reactions of the two women, either to the departure of their beloveds or to their new lovers' repeated advances, lie falsehood and deceit. This is made evident through the exaggerated, overstated reactions, from both literary and musical points of view. This was already clear in the finale of act 1, when the two sisters, after tragically displaying their horror and rejection of the intruders, ended up approaching them and even touching them. In reality, however, hypocrisy had already been hinted at in some of the earlier numbers in act 1: in the ensembles no. 6 (quintetto "Sento O Dio") and no. 13 (sestetto "Alla bella Despinetta"), and especially in the two *infuriate* arias of the protagonists, Dorabella's "Smanie implacabili" (no. 11) and Fiordiligi's "Come scoglio" (no. 14).

The quintet "Sento O Dio" takes place in scene 4. It involves the four original lovers plus Don Alfonso, who has just told the ladies the terrible news that their fiancés must leave for war. After the mandatory love protests, Ferrando and Guglielmo's asides ("Cosa dici?" "Te n'avvedi?"—What do you say now? Don't you see?), answered also in asides by Don Alfonso (*"Finem lauda"*—The applause at the end), remind us that, at least on their part, the whole number is a pretense, a lie. But what about the women? Their reactions, especially from bar 36 onwards ("A, no, no, no, non partirai! / No, crudel, non te n'andrai! / Voglio pria cavarmi il core! /Pria ti vo' morire ai piedi!"),[53] are stereotypes, of course, but they are also overblown, and the music we hear is exaggerated. That overstatement, that out-of-place style, is revealed in the abrupt textural and dynamic change: from a light, piano, intermittent accompaniment to a sudden string attack, which envelops the singing of these four verses like a storm, with rapid figurations and accents in the first part of each bar.

Later, in the sestetto "Alla bella Despinetta" in scene 11, in which the whole cast of the opera takes part, we witness the first occasion on which the

EXAMPLE 17. Bars 84–99, sestetto "Alla bella Despinetta," act 1, scene 11, no. 15

two friends, now disguised, begin to flatter the women. At the beginning of the number, and before the two sisters meet the strangers, Don Alfonso asks Despina, who is unaware that they are really Guglielmo and Ferrando, what she thinks about their looks. She replies that "Per parlavi schietto, schietto, hanno un muso fuor dell'uso, vero antidoto d'amor" (To be frank, they have unusual faces, the very antidote to love). It is interesting that, just before the deceitful plan is first hatched, Despina is encouraged to speak her mind, telling the truth as she sees it. She may perhaps be emphasizing that it makes no difference what they look like, because they will not be desirable for any objective reasons; they will not be chosen for their own sake (the object of desire has no value per se, according to Girard), but simply because they are a new object of desire, something the two women do not have and, if prompted in the right direction, will want to possess.

The sestetto introduction is followed by an Allegro in ternary meter (bar 54) when the two sisters enter the scene. The two men begin their attack (bar 82), always singing together, in a trio with Despina, declaring themselves to be passionate admirers ("spasimanti adorator"). Mozart captures this moment with a brief parenthesis, a special contrasting section (Example 17). The strings are silenced, and the instrumental accompaniment is reduced to clarinets and bassoons. From C major it moves to its relative minor, and the melody, in trochaic rhythm, is dominated by chromatic descents. The object of desire is presented, therefore, in a conveniently humiliated and servile manner.

As might be expected, Fiordiligi and Dorabella react by rejecting the strangers' advances. But it is an exaggerated rejection, in terms of both the language they use, claiming that their souls are full "di dispetto e di terror" (of spite and terror), and, above all, the music. Exaggeration can be insinuated musically, for example, by adopting a tragic style in a situation that is not tragic. With the return of the strings in repeated fast notes in crescendo, the rising melody, and the fast-descending scales in the final Molto Allegro, Mozart has designed such an exaggerated expression of rejection that it causes doubt to creep in: It is so extreme, so sudden and out of place, that it produces mistrust. In fact, this is verbally confirmed at the end of the number, when the other characters (Ferrando, Guglielmo, Don Alfonso, and Despina) explicitly declare that "so much anger and fury" make me "a little suspicious" ("Mi dà un poco si sospetto quella rabia e quel furor"). In other words, Mozart is suggesting that although the two sisters are saying "no," they are thinking "yes," and that, despite appearances, the flame of desire and curiosity may already have been lit inside them.

There is something else worth highlighting in this ending, which has less to do with the expression of hypocrisy and instead reveals the violence caused by the closeness of the double rivals. After having listened throughout the sextet to the two groups expressing themselves antagonistically, and separately, as is normal in musical numbers of this kind, at the end, as is also normal, the two sides are presented together, united in violent opposition: They display their two irreconcilable standpoints simultaneously and with the same music, singing homophonically, but with contrasting meanings:

> FL & DR: "Tutte piena ho l'alma in petto / di dispetto e di terror"
> GL, FD, DP & DA: "Mi dà un poco si sospetto / quella rabia e quel furor"

The audience behold a never-ending battle of great intensity, as—musically speaking—there are no winners, nor can there be. Everyone sings loudly, but none of the characters manage to impose themselves on the others. As they are all singing to exactly the same music, their voices become confused, blending together. It is easy to achieve this kind of experience through music, especially vocal music, and indeed it is part of what every opera lover expects from an ensemble number. However, it could also be seen as an expression, or at least a metaphor, for the escalating spiral towards violence that, according to Girard, is produced by the blurring of differences. It is difficult to know whether Mozart intended to show this; he probably did not, but at the same time it is hard to imagine a more effective way of musically expressing the equalization of rivalries, which in mimetic theory can lead to a total violent conflict, than by means of a combined swarm of equal voices—a polyphony in homophonic texture—singing texts with diametrically opposed meanings.

Let us return now to observing the exaggeration or parody of serious style in this opera, to the inklings of hypocrisy that lie behind the expression of feelings. The two clearest examples are in the arias sung respectively by Dorabella and Fiordiligi in act 1. Dorabella's aria "Smanie implacabili" (scene 9, no. 11) is intended to show the affection that overwhelms her after her fiancé's departure for the war. Instead of a lament, this aria offers a mockery of the serious style of infernal arias, a "supreme parody of distraught operatic passion," in the words of Steptoe.[54] The mockery is perceived in both text and music. The stereotyped poetic images presented are commonly used in other situations and here seem out of place. These include, for example, references to "amor funesto" (fatal love), the Furies or Eumenides, or the sighs conveyed in "suono orribile" (horrible sound). They are, according to Steptoe, "grandiose vehicles for fragile, transient feelings."[55] Musically, everything combines to create a strange, exaggerated perception, from the

EXAMPLE 18. Bars 70–73, aria "Smanie implacabili," act 1, scene 9, no. 11

vocal melody, intermittent and full of crazy intervallic jumps, to the insistent triplet accompaniment of the strings, in contrast with the prolonged chords of the woodwinds, often in crescendo, that recreate the "suono orribile" (e.g., in bars 71–73, Example 18).[56] The overstated style also reveals something about Dorabella's exaggerated, slightly pompous personality, incapable of elegance or perhaps just plain hysterical. In fact, according to Steptoe, in this aria Mozart is hinting that Dorabella may be mad (*smania*).

When assessing the degree of sincerity in the different numbers in this opera, it is important to bear in mind that the parodying of serious styles was an intrinsic feature of opera buffa. Hunter (1991) defines this genre as "fundamentally intertextual," in that it is composed of a recognizable combination of musical, textual, and dramatic elements, many of which derive from opera

EXAMPLE 19. Bars 54–59, aria "Come scoglio," act 1, scene 11, no. 14

seria. Specifically, among the usual parodies of serious stylistic genres, Hunter cites the scenes of feigned madness and the fury aria.[57] "Musically," she states, "such numbers are indistinguishable from their counterparts in *opera seria.* Dramatically, their evaluation as heroic, mock-heroic or pale imitation of heroic depends on the status of the character."[58] Therefore, if we take into account Dorabella's status within the plot as a buffo character, there can be no doubt as to the parodic intentions of the lines she sings, especially in an aria like "Smanie implacabili." Fiordiligi, however, is a much more complex character and is therefore more difficult to analyze.

Fiordiligi's recitative and aria in act 1, scene 11 (no. 14, "Come scoglio"), take place just after the two disguised friends make their passionate declaration of love, which began with a sextet and continued with a recitativo *accompagnato*, as discussed earlier. Fiordiligi brings the recitative to an end in a special Allegro section (bar 44) that leaves no doubt as to the firmness with which she rebuffs all the flattery and amorous declarations she has heard. This is confirmed by the strings with an affirmative, dotted ascending motive that is repeated several times as an echo of her voice. However, in bars 56 and 58, a completely different motif can be heard (Example 19): In bar 56, in reply to her reference to "L'intatta fede" (The unbroken fidelity), the first violins repeat, four times, an insinuating dotted motif on the same note on which she ended her phrase, A-flat, mockingly questioning her alleged determination and the apparent solidity of her fidelity. Just in case there was any doubt, the same motif is repeated two measures later, echoing the phrase "che per noi già si diede" (that was given for us). It is just one moment in the middle of a very affirmative section, which might go unnoticed by the audience. However, an intentional, deliberate emphasis by the musicians could give this passage a mocking tone, anticipating what is to come.

Fiordiligi's next aria is her *aria di sortita*, the first important number she sings in the opera and her first solo. According to the conventions of the operatic genre, it should show the full scope of the technical and expressive qualities of her voice, and this is indeed a very difficult number for the singer. Mozart uses all the musical weapons of this voice, including dizzying agility and rapid register changes, to raise the tone of angry rejection. The text, for its part, is categorical in its images of steadfastness and resistance, to the point of asserting that "la morte sola" (only death) would be able to sway the affections of the girl's heart. However, leading scholars of this opera, including Kramer, Rodney Farnsworth, Rosen, Kunze, Steptoe, Brown, Lewy, and Goehring, disagree as to the meaning of the aria, in the sense of whether Fiordiligi's expression is to be taken literally.[59] They fall into two main camps. On the one hand, there are those who think that the aria is a parody of the serious style and is therefore making fun of Fiordiligi's expressed wishes. If this were so, the more she claims that she will remain true "like a rock," the less we should believe it. This analysis is supported, for example, by Rosen, for whom the aria is insincere in contrast to the duet in which Fiordiligi finally yields, which for Rosen is a more genuine reflection of her feelings.[60] Lewy agrees, arguing that the aria is a burlesque portrayal of Fiordiligi, written to ridicule the style of the singer (Adriana Ferrarese del Bene) for whom it was written.[61] Even Brown explains the details that he believes make it evident that this aria is, musically, a parody of Fiordiligi's real feelings.[62] In essence, he argues that however much Fiordiligi may want to believe what she is singing, the music is telling us that none of what she says will actually happen. In the opposing camp, there are those who argue that Mozart, even to the point of correcting Da Ponte, has created an aria that is in no way parodic and instead offers a genuine expression of sincere feelings. Hunter, for example, proposes the aria "Come scoglio" as an example of the way Mozart treats the Fiordiligi character seriously.[63] I have already noted how Mozart seems to dispense with parody in the rondo "Per pietà" and in the duet that she sings with her new lover in act 2, in which all we see is Fiordiligi's truth, her inner struggle. While listening to this music, we have even a suspicion of a brief "betrayal" by Mozart of his critique of (unintentional) human hypocrisy that runs through *Così*. According to Hunter, "musical context rather than content almost always determines the tone of the moment," so that "Come scoglio" "must be interpreted in the light of what it means for Fiordiligi at this moment to sing a simile aria in elevated style."[64] Clearly for Fiordiligi it means that she is determined to be firm, at least for the moment, and that she is serious about it. Steptoe positions himself somewhere between these two extremes, when he claims that the aria is "the epitome of *seria* fortitude in adversity," albeit designed "as a parody of the archetypal exit aria."[65] For him, Mozart's music is not a complete caricature; it begins as such in the first two lines, which speak of the firm rock facing the storm, but the next two, which deal with the strong and faithful soul, are more intimate and personal, less archetypal, and are treated more gently and more fondly. Then, in the reprise of the opening bars, the composer returns to the parodic style. Steptoe argues that these stylistic changes show that "in Mozart's music, the sincerity and vulnerability at the heart of Fiordiligi's prayer is not completely disguised by satire."[66]

Once again, we are faced with a dilemma: Which of these interpretations is correct? The answer is important, not only for this particular study, but also when it comes to singing the aria. Whichever option is taken regarding the genuineness or otherwise of Fiordiligi's feelings will necessarily influence the singer's performance, both vocally and dramatically. Personally, I am more inclined to view it, as Steptoe does, as a generally serious piece with some parodic features. A serious musical interpretation of the resolute indignation that drives Fiordiligi, such as that performed by the soprano Cecilia Bartoli in the version of the opera recorded by Nikolaus Harnoncourt for HartHaus Musik label in 2000, allows us to observe the powerful influence that imitation can have on others, in this case on Dorabella. As Fiordiligi sings her aria, she helps convince her sister, almost seducing her with her firmness. Is this moment not a replica, a copy of the resistance shown by other heroines, such as Procris or Camilla, from the sources on which the libretto draws? What better way could Mozart have of representing Fiordiligi's initial resistance than by inserting a serious scene into an opera buffa? Those who argue that, in this aria, Mozart is parodying Fiordiligi's determination to remain true are not taking into account the traditional fable or story on which the libretto is based, in which this scene needs to be serious. The woman who intones her fidelity is a victim of her own belief in the lies of immovable, romantic, or absolute love. She is as yet unaware that she will fail; it does not even cross her mind, which explains why it is necessary and urgent that she enroll in Mozart's "scuola degli amanti" (school for lovers). In short, "Come scoglio," and perhaps also the rondo "Per pietà" and even the love duet with Ferrando, should not be considered as "romantic" slips on Mozart's part, but rather as the sincere expression of certain beliefs. The opera will gradually demonstrate how false these beliefs really are.

Fiordiligi's ignorance as to the falsity of her beliefs could be related to the Girardian concept of *méconnaissance* (ignorance, unawareness). The bearers of desire are unconscious or unaware of their real desires, and they therefore express themselves as if these desires did not exist, even though their actions seem focused on achieving them. In my opinion, Kunze noticed this in *Così fan tutte* when he stated that "with the exception of Don Alfonso and Despina, the characters often give us the impression of not knowing or not noticing what is happening to them and how."[67] "In *Così fan tutte* it is not a question of guilt, or in other words, guilt is explicitly excluded. . . . Indeed, Don Alfonso makes clear that the girls act in accordance with nature." It is not their frivolity or weakness that causes the damage, but rather "the foolish decision to hold the fidelity test."[68] It is foolish because it is doomed to fail, as Don Alfonso well knows, and it will inevitably cause harm because it is guided by a mad (*pazzo*) desire, in this case unconscious mimetic desire.

In short, we have seen how extreme reactions to situations that would normally arouse a calmer, less embellished response can be understood as exaggerated or directly hypocritical. They can also be interpreted as apparently sincere, despite in fact being, sometimes unknowingly, false. This falsehood may be unconscious or even overtly hypocritical, but in a comedy it must be obvious that it contains no authentic elements. A powerful way of making this clear is to emphasize the falsehood by exaggerating the way the characters express themselves. In opera buffa, this inappropriate, overblown response is essentially produced using musical resources, both vocal and instrumental. In the case of *Così fan tutte*, the expression of amorous feelings can only be false because the premise is that there is no such thing as absolute enduring love, as Don Alfonso has been claiming all along. *Così* will not fall into the romantic lie, but will strive to reveal the novelistic truth, both in moments of parody and when we are privy to the expression, experienced as true, of feelings such as rejection, regret, or passion. Steptoe captured this intention perfectly: "The underlying purpose of the entire plot is to disprove the romantic, idealistic convention that lovers are made for each other, and that passion is immutable."[69]

Disappointment and Reconciliation in the Final Outcome

The ending of *Così fan tutte* takes place in two phases. The first centers on the revelation of the truth, and the second on the original couples being reunited and "happily" reconciled. The first phase begins just after Fiordiligi's surrender, the moment in which the two friends intone, together with Don Alfonso, the saying after which the opera is named. The two sisters, however, will still have to go through the masquerade of the fake wedding before they discover what has really been going on. When they find out that they have been duped, when they discover that the gallantries were false, the balance within their daily lives is shattered and their first reaction is anger, which perhaps hides a feeling of shame. At this point, Girard's words on the mechanisms of *marivaudage*—in other words, the way in which Marivaux reveals the deceptions of vanity in his comedies—are enlightening and can teach us how to interpret the reactions of the two women when their hypocrisy and self-deception is unveiled: "*Marivaudage* . . . is an attempt to reveal the process of half-unconscious self-delusion at the very moment it is taking place and from the perspective of the half-deluded subject himself"; "the tricks with which a character manages to deceive himself become quite transparent to him when they are employed by others."[70] Indeed, Dorabella and Fiordiligi are furious when they discover the trickery. However, their anger and shame spring from their becoming aware that they have been deceiving themselves, which has also been made public. Everything is now out in the open, nothing is hidden from view.

But Girard goes even further by reflecting on a happy ending that comes after the devastation produced by the revelation of the truth. This is the case of Marivaux's comedies, which, like opera buffa, by convention require a *lieto fine*, or happy ending. Girard explains how skillful Marivaux is at revealing on stage the hypocrisy of vanities, and how this hypocrisy is alleviated, but not expunged, by the theatrical conventions of the time:

> The "happy ending" is demanded by the genre of the comedy. The conventions of the theater disguise somewhat, but do not suppress the ruthless character of Marivaudian *amour-propre*. . . . What concludes the amorous battle is really an alliance between the rival *vanités*, and the mutual admiration society thus formed looks plausible enough as a substitute for requited love so long as its durability does not have to be tested; we can be sure, of course, that no such test is forthcoming, since the play is at an end.[71]

And what if such a test were to be held? This is exactly what happens in *Così*: The durability of these alliances is put to the test. *Così* begins where other works end, with two young couples seemingly destined to live happily ever after. In *Così*, however, this happiness is shattered by the test, a test proposed by the male members of the couples. Ultimately, the opera does indeed have its own "happy ending," but it is of course a complete disaster. The original couples are finally reunited. While at the beginning they appeared to be genuine, after the test we know they are quite the opposite. No wonder the opera was rejected almost immediately after it was first performed. It was too real, too raw. This negative view of the ending of *Così fan tutte* still finds favor among many scholars. These include Ford, Natošević, Cochran, and Giuseppe Gazzola, for whom the opera does away with all romantic illusion, embodied above all in Fiordiligi.[72] They argue that its ending makes forgiveness impossible, given that the love between the original couples has been destroyed with the cynical collaboration of Don Alfonso and Despina. Apparently, from this point of view there is a hidden prejudice or assumption, shared by quite a number of scholars, that materialism should be regarded as negative, as opposed to idealism, which is always positive, a fact beyond debate. However, from Girard's point of view, it is idealism that has the most negative aspects or consequences, because it is based on a falsehood—on the romantic lie that certain works of art, of which I believe *Così fan tutte* is one, are determined to unmask.

In fact, the "happy" ending to *Così fan tutte* is not completely bereft of hope. The disappointment suffered by the two couples is not nihilistic and instead is based, as Moindrot asserts, on "the recognition of the illusion that, beyond the changing stream of appearances, allows us to glimpse a serene image of the eternal."[73] The final words of the opera invite us to let reason guide us so that we can find serenity "del mondo in mezzo i turbini" (in the midst of the whirlwinds of the world), which is nothing but a false illusion.

Moindrot affirms that this false illusion comes from the fact that the human being is mortal and finite. I believe that it may be a product of the fundamental law of mimetic desire, which is a direct consequence of the finiteness or incompleteness of the human being.

The truth is that most researchers agree in offering a positive interpretation of the ending of the opera and therefore of its meaning. For example, Kramer follows the theory put forward by Gombrich, according to which Da Ponte's intention in his libretto is to "propose a rational form of behavior based on humanity," such that in the end there is "rational forgiveness as a principle for resolving the tragic conflict."[74] Similarly, Hunter proclaimed that the ending of *Così fan tutte* offers an "enlightened ethos of reconciling reason and desire, . . . a lesson in wisdom to be learned from clear-eyed acceptance of what is given."[75] Farnsworth and, in particular, Goehring could also be added to this list. Farnsworth makes a heated defense of Don Alfonso, "the rational man," "standing like a rock amid a wash of human silliness,"[76] while Goehring considers *Così* not as a coldly rationalist work but as an antisentimental one, in that Don Alfonso takes the lovers "from sentimental confidence to a comic recognition and acceptance of fallibility."[77] In general, all these authors end up seeing Don Alfonso as a model of pragmatic wisdom, rather than the cold, cruel individual that some scholars of the opera choose to cast him as.[78]

This positive view of the opera's conclusion can be explained by Girard's analysis of the endings of various literary classics, including *Don Quijote*, the episode of Paolo and Francesca in *The Divine Comedy*, and *A Midsummer Night's Dream*. In these works, the final conversion of the hero secures his liberation from mimetic desire and in this sense is always a happy ending. That is to say, happiness does not come from carrying on living, but from living or dying while being fully aware of the truth about human desire. When Don Quijote is dying, he regains his sanity and undergoes a conversion in which he rejects the desire by mediation that has led him to commit so many follies. The hero recognizes "the vanity and degraded character of not only the previous quest, but also of any hope, of any possible quest."[79] When Francesca explains to Dante how the desire that led them to hell sprung unconsciously from an act of imitation of Lancelot and Guinevere, the poet exclaims before her: "How much desire, conducted these unto the dolorous pass!" (Dante 5.113–114).[80] The characters in *A Midsummer Night's Dream* realize that they have undergone "a collective ordeal, and, ultimately a kind of initiation ritual that they all successfully complete."[81] In short, to arrive at an authentic, sane, lucid vision of the self, one has to undergo a process of "renunciation of his own idols," rejection of "desire by mediation," and "death of the romantic self." In this way, "the final revelation illuminates, retrospectively, the path traversed," a path that involves "the necessary ordeal on the way to final revelation."[82] These are the words that Girard uses to refer to the denouements of various literary works of mimetic revelation, but they seem to have been written expressly to describe the ending of *Così fan tutte*, or *La scuola degli amanti*.

After the revelation of the truth, which has shown that the values we believed to be true "have been relativized or subverted,"[83] our only option is to accept this situation and try to save ourselves through the rule of reason, which offers a sympathetic look at human weaknesses. Just as Cervantes looks kindly on Don Quijote by restoring his sanity so that he can fully comprehend the truth of his past madness and, in so doing, regain his dignity,[84] and just as Shakespeare in *The Winter's Tale* leads Leontes from the mimetic fever that has brought tragedy to his family to repentance and redemption,[85] so Mozart and Da Ponte heal the wounds of their damaged characters by showing them how to face the painful truth of their own fragility, as they sing these final verses together:

> Fortunato l'uom che prende
> ogni cosa pel buon verso,
> e tra i casi e le vicende
> da ragion guidar si fa.
> Quel che suole altrui far piangere
> fia per lui cagion di riso,
> e del mondo in mezzo ai turbini
> bella calma troverà.
>
> Fortunate is the man who takes
> everything in a good way,
> and among cases and events
> by reason he makes himself guided.
> That which is able to make others weep

shall be to him cause of laughter,
and of the world amid the whirlwinds
beautiful calm he will find.

Turning to Kunze's interpretation of the opera's ending, philosophical serenity, represented by Don Alfonso, is the remedy to recover "order in irreparable chaos."[86] Since "direct observation of human realities is often a source of unhappiness," philosophical serenity "means . . . the overcoming of the ephemeral agitation of the senses, the renunciation of amorous passion."[87] Kunze continues: "The nineteenth century, fascinated by the theme of amorous passion linked with destiny and doom, was unable to understand this theory. It was impossible for it to be true."[88] These insights make even more sense if we approach them from the perspective of Girardian theory. According to this theory, the happy ending can only be achieved by renouncing the desire to possess what other people have, a natural desire in human beings that we prefer not to admit we are prone to. The romantic lie is to believe that love and passion are real, when what is real is mimetic desire—, something that this opera, like the great literary works of Cervantes and Shakespeare, brings to light.

In the preceding pages I have closely analyzed *Così fan tutte* in a search for the moments in which the mechanisms of mimetic desire are revealed. I have examined how the words and actions and, especially, the music combine to expose these mechanisms. During this search, I have detected numerous elements of Girard's theory of mimetic desire, including the identicality of mimetic doubles, activation and incitement of desire, imitation, rivalry, hypocrisy and vanity (*marivaudage*), ignorance or lack of awareness (*méconnaissance*), contagious spread, unveiling of the truth, and final rational acceptance. Tables 10 and 11 show how these moments act as marker points on the journey through the opera, giving it structure. The tables include all of the different numbers in the opera, and those analyzed in detail in this book are marked in bold. The right-hand column shows the Girardian topics found in these numbers. The names of the characters have been abbreviated, as have the expressions "Male doubles" and "Female doubles," which appear as "M doubles" and "F doubles" respectively.

TABLE 10. Numbers from *Così fan tutte* act 1

ACT 1			
SCENE	**NUMBER**	**CHARACTER**	**TOPIC**
Overture			
Bottega 1	**no. 1** terzetto	FD/GL/DA	M doubles, activation of desire
	recitativo & no. 2 terzetto		
	recitativo & no. 3 terzetto		
Giardino 2	**no. 4** duetto "Ah guarda sorella"	FL/DR	F doubles, activation of desire
2 , 3	recitativo	FL/DR/DA	
3	no. 5 aria	DA	
	recitativo	FL/DR/DA	
4	**no. 6** quintetto "Sento O Dio"	FL/DR/DA/FD/GL	F doubles, exaggerated rejection and hypocrisy
	recitativo		
	no. 7 duettino "Al fato dàn legge"	FD/GL	M doubles, activation of desire
	recitativo		
5	no. 8 *coro* "Bella vita militar"		
	no. 8a quintetto "Di scrivermi"	FL/DR/DA/FD/GL	
	no. 9 *coro* "Bella vita militar"		
6	no. 10 *terzettino* "Soave sia il vento"	FL/DR/DA	
7	recitativo & arioso	DA	
Camera 8	recitativo	DP/DR/FL	
9	recitativo *accompagnatto*	DR	
	no. 11 aria "Smanie implacabili"	DR	DR, exaggerated rejection and hypocrisy

TABLE 10 (*continued*)

ACT 1			
SCENE	**NUMBER**	**CHARACTER**	**TOPIC**
	recitativo	DP	F doubles, incitement to desire and imitation
	no. 12 aria "In uomini, in soldati"	DP	
10	recitativo	DA/DP	
11	**no. 13** sestetto "Alla bella Despinetta"	tutti	F doubles, exaggerated rejection and hypocrisy
	recitativo-*recitativo accompagnato*	FD/GL	F doubles, incitement to desire
	recitativo accompagnato	FL	FL, serious rejection *¿Méconnaissance?*
	no. 14 aria "Come scoglio"	FL	
	recitativo	GL	
	no. 15 aria "Non siate ritrosi"	GL	F doubles, incitement to desire and vanity
12	no. 16 terzetto "E voi ridete?"	GL/ FD/DA	
	no. 17 aria "Un aura amorosa"	FD	
13	recitativo	DA/ DP	
Giardinetto 14	**no. 18 finale** duetto "Ah che tutte in un momento," andante 2/4	FL/DR	F doubles, hypocrisy and contagion
15	quintetto-quartetto, allegro 2/2	FL/DR/FD/GL/DA/ Poi DP	
16	quartetto, allegro 3/4	DP/DA/FL/DR	
	sestetto, andante 4/4	tutti	
	allegro 2/2	tutti	

Note: Numbers analyzed in chapter 5 appear in bold.

TABLE 11. Numbers from *Così fan tutte* act 2

ACT 2			
SCENE	**NUMBER**	**CHARACTER**	**TOPIC**
Camera 1	recitativo	DP/FL/DR	
	no. 19 aria, "Una donna"	DP	F doubles, incitement to desire and imitation
2	**recitativo**	FL/DR	F doubles, *marivaudage*
	no. 20 duetto "Prenderò quel brunettino"	FL/DR	
3	recitativo		
Giardino 4	**no. 21** duetto with coro "Secondate"	FD/GL/*coro*	F doubles, incitement to desire
	recitativo	Tutti	
	no. 22 quartetto "La mano a me date"	FD/GL/DP/DA	
5	recitativo	FD/GL/FL/DR	
	no. 23 duetto "Il core vi dono"	GL/DR	DR, yielding
6	***recitativo accompagnato***	FD/FL	FL, resistance
	no. 24 aria "A, lo veggio" [omitted]	FD	
7	***recitativo accompagnato*** (cont.)	FL	FL, resistance and repentance
	no. 25 aria-rondo "Per pietà"	FL	
8	**recitativo**	FD/ GL	M doubles, incitement to desire and rivalry
	recitativo accompagnato	FD/GL	
	no. 26 aria "Donne mie"	GL	
9	***recitativo accompagnato***	FD	M doubles, incitement to desire and rivalry
	no. 27 cavatina "Tradito, schernito"	FD	

TABLE 11 (*continued*)

ACT 2			
SCENE	**NUMBER**	**CHARACTER**	**TOPIC**
	recitativo	FD/ DA/GL	
Camera 10	**recitativo**	DP/DR/FL	F doubles, incitement to desire and imitation
	no. 28 aria "E amore un ladroncello"	DR	
11	recitativo	FL/DP/(GL)	
12	**recitativo**	FL/ FD/(GL/DA)	FL, resistance and surrender
	no. 29 duetto "Fra gli amplessi"	FL/FD	
13	**recitativo**	GL/DA/FD/(DP)	M doubles, unveiling of the truth
	no. 30 andante "Tutti acusan le donne"	DA	
14	recitativo	DP	
Sala 15	no. 31 finale allegro assai 4/4	DP/DA/*coro*	
16	andante 2/2	*coro*/tutti	
	andante 2/2	FD/GL/FL/DR	
	larghetto 3/4	FL/FD/DR/GL	
17	allegro 2/2	tutti	
	maestoso 2/2	*coro*	
	allegro 3/4–2/2	tutti	
18	andante 2/2, allegro 2/2	FD/GL	
	andante 2/2	FL/DR	
	allegretto 2/2	FD	
	andante 3/8	GL	
	allegretto 3/8	FD/GL	
	andante con moto 2/2	DA	F doubles, unveiling of the truth
	allegro molto 2/2	tutti	disillusion and acceptance

Note: Numbers analyzed in chapter 5 appear in bold

EPILOGUE

Revealing the Truth of Human Emotions

THIS STUDY SPRANG FROM AN INTUITION: IF SOME SOURCES OF THE libretto for *Così fan tutte* have been interpreted from a Girardian perspective and can therefore be considered bearers of novelistic truth, can the same claims be made about the opera itself? In other words, does *Così* seek to reveal, through its words, actions, and music, the truth about the mechanisms of mimetic desire as theorized by René Girard? Much has been written about this opera, but to the best of my knowledge, this particular question had never been addressed. Girard himself never investigated the opera genre, although he did reference some operatic works, including a specific mention of *Così fan tutte*. In the bibliography consulted in this research, there are many ideas and interpretations that seem to coincide with those of Girard and that have tended to confirm my own intuition. However, there is also quite a wide diversity of views regarding the meaning of some numbers or scenes in the opera. All these authors analyze the feelings expressed by the different characters, trying to establish which are genuine and which are false, and coming to quite distinct conclusions. Where some find pretense, irony, or parody, others find sincerity. Among the latter are Rosen, Farnsworth, Steptoe, Brèque, Moindrot, Hunter, and Goehring.[1] In my opinion, the most insightful and accurate comments were provided by Kunze. For him, Mozart's music "takes

Ferrando's love and Dorabella and Fiordiligi's despair seriously, and envelops the situations . . . with the aura of truth and intimacy."[2] According to him, even passages in the libretto that were surely conceived by Da Ponte as ironic or parodic (such as "Smanie implacabili" by Dorabella or "Come scoglio" by Fiordiligi) were developed by Mozart in a "categorically serious" way.[3] "*Così fan tutte*—he states—is a (dangerous) game with the natural laws of the human heart, a scientific experiment in the form of a comedy. It deals with nothing less than the mechanical laws of love."[4] Having analyzed the opera through the prism of Girardian theory, I can now add that the human laws *Così fan tutte* seeks to demonstrate are the laws of mimetic desire. Its double characters move from identification to rivalry; they are invaded by desires they never expected to encounter; they believe, naively, that they can ignore them; and finally they surrender in the face of their own weakness.

The fact that this is demonstrated in a comedy further enhances its effectiveness. In an essay on comedy published in 1972,[5] Girard takes a highly perceptive look at its capacity to reveal the truth. He argues that comedy, and not just tragedy, is a very appropriate genre for unveiling the mechanism of mimetic desire. He asserts that "the crisis element is more acute in laughter than in tears,"[6] in that laughter is a mechanism of expulsion, which expresses the group's rejection of the person they are laughing at and generates purification. Within comedy, this purification is experienced by the characters who have suffered the consequences of their own actions, the ultimate revelation of the truth of their desires, as is evident in the ending of *Così fan tutte.*[7] Internal spectators, characters defined by their wisdom about human behavior, can also achieve purification. In *Così fan tutte* this role is played by Don Alfonso. "The spectator's position," Girard affirms, "is one of austere moral pessimism and satiric glee over human foibles. The spectacle of human frailty has an exhilarating as well as a depressing effect upon the moralist." Our moralist, Don Alfonso, as both a promoter and spectator of the test, fears what is going to happen while enjoying the spectacle of his friends' weakness. But, Girard adds, "This spectator's position is not his only, but our own as well, since we are the spectators of the play."[8] Indeed, at the end of the opera, both the characters and the audience are forced to agree with Don Alfonso. Having learned the lessons offered by this opera regarding our inherent frailty, we can now be sure that, put to the test, "so would we all."

Notes

Preface

1. Cesáreo Bandera, *"Monda y desnuda," la humilde historia de Don Quijote* (Madrid: Editorial Iberoamericana, 2005).

2. René Girard, *Mentira romántica y verdad novelesca* (Barcelona: Anagrama, 1985) 49ff.

3. For example, regarding Shakespeare's *The Rape of Lucrece*, "More than ever we see that mimetic desire is no alien entity in the work of Shakespeare; it is not a 'critical tool' that I, the critic, would be *applying* to this work from the outside"; and later in the same chapter, Girard asks himself the following fundamental question: "What does this poem teach us about his conception of desire, and about our own?" René Girard, *A Theater of Envy: William Shakespeare* (Oxford: Oxford University Press, 1991), 23–25.

4. This approach came from reading Berry Vorstenbosch's article "Against the Grain: Mimetic Theory and the Case of Boris Godunov" (Girard studiekring-Dutch Girard Society, n.d. [2009?]). Retrieved from https://www.girard.nl/texts_online/v/Vorstenbosch_Berry_2.pdf.

Chapter 1. Creation and Reception of *Così fan tutte*

1. While searching through the Austrian National Library Music Collection, which holds the largest volume of Salieri's scores, Rice discovered some sheet music in Salieri's own hand for the first two numbers of the libretto. It also seems logical that the libretto, which has many classical literary influences, was originally intended for

Salieri, who was more cultivated than Mozart. See Bruce Alan Brown and John A. Rice, "Salieri's 'Così fan tutte,'" *Cambridge Opera Journal* 8, 1 (March 1996): 20, 25. See also Simon P. Keefe, *Mozart in Vienna: The Final Decade* (Cambridge: Cambridge University Press, 2017), 415; Christoph Wolff, *Mozart en el umbral de su plenitud. Al servicio del emperador (1788–1791)* (Barcelona: Acantilado, 2018), 70–71.

2. Wolff, *Mozart en el umbral, 68* [*author's translation*].

3. As is well known, Mozart linked the three words of the title to a specific musical motif, which first appears in the Overture and then crops up again towards the end of the opera, sung by the male characters. From the very beginning, Mozart and Da Ponte are making clear what the outcome will be. It is also interesting to note that exactly the same expression had been used in their previous opera *Le nozze di Figaro*, in this case sung by the cynical music teacher (Act I, trio "Cosa sento"). It is significant that while Da Ponte always referred to the opera by its original title, *La scuola degli amanti*, Mozart insisted on calling it *Così fan tutte*, repeatedly emphasizing the importance of this expression in his music. For a more in-depth analysis of the Overture and the meaning of the "Così fan tutte" motif, see Edmund J. Goehring, *Three Modes of Perception in Mozart: The Philosophical, Pastoral, and Comic in* Così fan tutte (Cambridge: Cambridge University Press, 2004), 42–52.

4. See, for example, Kurt Kramer, "Da Pontes Così fan tutte," *Nachrichten der Akademie der Wissenschaften in Göttingen,* 1. *Philologisch-historische Klasse* 1 (1973), 3–27; Daniel Heartz, "Mozart and Da Ponte," *Musical Quarterly* 79, 4 (Winter 1995), 700–718; and Pierpaolo Polzonetti, "Mesmerizing Adultery: *Così fan tutte* and the Kornman Scandal," *Cambridge Opera Journal* 14, 3 (2002), 263–296.

5. Contrary to what has always been assumed, there is no trace in the sources of a possible commission from the emperor. The first author to make this clear was Kurt Kramer, in 1973. See also Andrew Steptoe, "The Sources of 'Così fan tutte': A Reappraisal," *Music & Letters* 62, 3/4 (1981), 281; Bruce Alan Brown, *W. A. Mozart Così fan tutte* (Cambridge: Cambridge University Press, 1995), 9–10; Goehring, *Three Modes*, 3; and Wolff, *Mozart en el umbral*, 68–71.

6. Wolff, *Mozart en el umbral*, 71.

7. Keefe, *Mozart in Vienna,* 417.

8. See Dexter Edge, "Mozart's Fee for *Così fan tutte*," *Journal of the Royal Musical Association* 116 (1991): 211–235. According to Edge, Mozart wrote in a letter to his friend Puchberg that he expected to be paid 900 gulden (200 ducats) for *Così*, but ledgers from the Burgtheater for the years 1789–1790 reveal that, in the end, he only received 450 gulden, in 1790 in a single payment. The same sources also make clear that he did not receive any additional special gifts. If Mozart was promised anything else, he never received it, perhaps due to spending cuts as a result of the war with the Turks or to the illness and premature death of the emperor preventing him from making any further payments of a personal nature. It may even have been due to Salieri plotting against Mozart. In short, if indeed he should have been paid more for *Così*, which is a possibility, it would seem that, as Edge says, in this case "Mozart was a victim of circumstance" (235).

9. Keefe, *Mozart in Vienna*, 441ff.

10. Keefe, *Mozart in Vienna*, 442.

11. Edmund Goehring takes us on an interesting journey through the history of the negative opinions about *Così fan tutte* since it was first performed. He also provides a study of how the opera was received in the eighteenth century, including documentary evidence about the number of people who saw the show, before finally concluding that its initial reception was in fact quite good. He then puts forward various possible reasons for its subsequent fall from grace, among which he highlights the poor quality of the translations of the libretto into German. See Goehring, *Three Modes*, 1–28.

12. Alfred Einstein, *Mozart: His Character, His Work* (New York: Oxford University Press, 1945); Edward Joseph Dent, *Mozart's Operas: A Critical Study* (2nd edition, London: Oxford University Press, 1947).

13. Keefe, *Mozart in Vienna*, 442ff.

14. For bibliography on the sources of the libretto, see chapter 3.

15. Charles Rosen, *El estilo clásico: Haydn, Mozart, Beethoven* (Madrid: Alianza Editorial, 1999).

16. Isabelle Moindrot, "Così fan tutte ou les artifices de l'idéal," *Così fan tutte. L'Avant scène opéra* 131–132 (mai-juin, 1990): 23–34.

17. Jean-Michel Brèque, "Prima la musica, dopo le parole," *Così fan tutte. L'Avant scène opéra* 131–132 (mai-juin, 1990): 146–157.

18. Brown, *W. A. Mozart Così fan tutte*, 70ff.

19. Mary Hunter, "*Così fan tutte* et les conventions musicaux de son temps," *Così fan tutte. L'Avant scène opéra* 131–132 (mai-juin,1990): 158–64; Mary Hunter, *The Culture of Opera Buffa in Mozart's Vienna: A Poetics of Entertainment* (Princeton Studies in Opera, 13. Princeton, N.J.: Princeton University Press, 1999).

20. Stefan Kunze, *Las óperas de Mozart* (Madrid: Alianza Editorial, 1990); Andrew Steptoe, *Mozart-Da Ponte Operas: The Cultural and Musical Background to Le Nozze Di Figaro, Don Giovanni, and Così Fan Tutte* (Oxford: Clarendon Paperbacks, 1990).

21. Charles Ford, *Così? Sexual Politics in Mozart's Operas* (Manchester: Manchester University Press, 1991); Charles Ford, *Music, Sexuality and the Enlightenment in Mozart's Figaro, Don Giovanni and Così fan tutte* (Farnham, U.K.: Ashgate, 2012).

22. The astonishing number of publications in 1990 is perhaps not as surprising as it might first appear, if we take into account that the articles by Moindrot, Brèque, and Hunter appeared in the same issue of *L'Avant scène opéra* devoted to *Così fan tutte*. In addition, although Kunze's and Steptoe's books on Mozart's operas were originally published in 1984 and 1988 respectively, in this study I cite the Spanish translation of Kunze's book and the 2nd edition of Steptoe's book, both of which appeared in 1990.

23. A brief explanation of these two fundamental concepts, presented by Girard in his first book (*Mensonge romantique et vérité romanesque*, 1961), can be found in chapter 4.

Chapter 2. Summary of the Plot and Structural Relationships

1. Wolff, *Mozart en el umbral*, 41.

2. If we bear in mind that the Austrian Empire had already been at war with the Ottoman Empire for three years when the opera premiered, we can imagine that the audience at the first performances in Vienna must have felt especially involved in the farce, both during this scene when they are bidding farewell and later when the seducers disguise themselves as exotic "Albanians" to carry out their plan.

3. The name of this object came from the physician Franz Mesmer (1734–1815) and his "mesmerism" therapy based on magnetism. Ever since Kramer discovered that Dr. Mesmer was a close friend of Mozart's family, it has been suggested that this may be why a scene on mesmerism was included in the libretto. However, the way in which Mozart and Da Ponte make fun of this supposed healing method, by inserting the scene in a particularly farcical section of the opera that is also a turning point in the story, has led some researchers to analyze this reference to mesmerism in more detail. See Goehring, *Three Modes*, 90ff., and Polzonetti, "Mesmerizing Adultery."

4. Brown, *W. A. Mozart Così fan tutte*, 95: "There is no demonstration of male inconstancy equivalent to the test the women are put through. . . . In any case the decision had crucial repercussions for the structure and working-out of *Così*."

5. Created after an idea of Brown, *W. A. Mozart Così fan tutte*, 96.

6. Heartz, "Mozart and Da Ponte," 709. See also Daniel Heartz, *Mozart's Operas* (Berkeley: University of California Press, 1990).

7. Constanze Natošević, "*Così fan tutte*": *Mozart, die Liebe und die Revolution von 1789* (Kassel, Germany: Bärenreiter, 2003). This researcher asserted that themes like these were associated with the revolutionary spirit of the time: While faithfulness represented order, infidelity destroyed it.

8. Steptoe, *Mozart-Da Ponte Operas*, 132.

9. Steptoe, *Mozart-Da Ponte Operas*, 133.

10. José Luis Téllez, "¿Sólo un cuento (in)moral?" in *Così fan tutte. Teatro Real. Temporada 2001–2002* (Madrid: Fundación del Teatro Lírico, 2001), 124–126 [*author's translation*].

Chapter 3. The Literary Sources of the Libretto

1. Ernst H. Gombrich, "Così fan tutte (Procris Included)," *Journal of the Warburg Courtauld Institutes* xvii (1954): 372–374.

2. Within the vast bibliography on *Così fan tutte*, the following publications focus particularly on the question of the sources for the libretto: Gombrich, "Così fan tutte (Procris Included)"; Ann Livermore, "'Così fan tutte': A Well-Kept Secret," *Music & Letters* 46, 4 (1965): 316–321; Kramer, "Da Pontes Così fan tutte"; Steptoe ,"The Sources of 'Così fan tutte'"; Brian Robins, "Così and Ariosto," *Musical Times* 123,

1676 (October 1982): 666; Kunze, *Las óperas de Mozart;* Marc Vignal, "Sources, composition et créateurs," *Così fan tutte. L'Avant scène opéra* 131–132 (mai-juin 1990): 6–15; Daniel Heartz, "Trois écoles des amants. *Così fan tutte,*" *L'Avant scène opéra* 131–132 (mai-juin, 1990): 16–22; Heartz, "Mozart and Da Ponte"; Mary Hunter, "Some Representations of Opera Seria in Opera Buffa," *Cambridge Opera Journal* 3, 2 (July 1991): 89–108; Hunter, *Culture of Opera Buffa in Mozart's Vienna*; Carlo Caruso, "'Così fan tutte,' o sia la scuola dell' 'Orlando furioso,'" *Il Saggiatore musicale* 1, 2 (1994): 361–375; Brown, *W. A. Mozart Così fan tutte*; Brown and Rice "Salieri's 'Così fan tutte'"; Dorothea Link, "*L'arbore di Diana*: A Model for *Così fan tutte,*" in *Wolfgang Amadè Mozart: Essays on His Life and His Music* (New York: Oxford University Press-Clarendon Press, 1996), 362–376; Raffaele Mellace, "Nel laboratorio di Da Ponte: *Così fan tutte, Le nozze di Figaro* e la librettistica coeva," *Rivista Italiana di Musicologia* 33, 2 (1998): 279–300; Goehring, *Three Modes*; Iole Scamuzzi, "Ovidio e Cervantes nella cultura di Da Ponte: alle radici del 'Così fan tutte,'" *Lettere Italiane* 56, 3 (2004): 468–483; Iole Scamuzzi, "Tra Bradamante e Fiordiligi c'è Camila: la novella del *Curioso Impertinente* come fonte del libretto di *Così Fan Tutte,*" *Artifara* 4 (2004): 211–221; Iole Scamuzzi, "*El curioso impertinente* de Cervantes: tragedia barroca y ópera buffa," in *Recreaciones teatrales y alegorías cervantinas* (Navarra, Spain: EUNSA-Publicaciones de literatura-Departamento de Filología, 2012), 135–141; Iole Scamuzzi, "Los dos amigos: Boccaccio, Cervantes, Guillén de Castro," in *Rumbos del hispanismo en el umbral del Cincuentenario de la Asociación Internacional de Hispanistas* (Roma: Bagatto Libri, 2012), 217–222; Peter Cochran, "Da Ponte, Mozart, Byron, Casti: A Question of Dimensions," in *Byron and Women (and Men)* (Newcastle: Cambridge Scholars, 2010), 125–145; Keefe, *Mozart in Vienna.*

3. According to Kramer ("Da Pontes Così fan tutte"), there is another Boccaccio tale that could also be seen as a possible source for *Così*. This is the story of Procris from his book *De claris mulieribus*. The link is especially clear in the way in which the Italian author insists that "avaritia e gelosia" (greed and jealousy) are the ultimate causes of the couple's misfortune.

4. Kramer, "Da Pontes Così fan tutte," and Brown, *W. A. Mozart Così fan tutte.*

5. It was a successful comparison, as it is also found in Tirso de Molina (*La celosa de sí misma*, 1621) and in Pietro Metastasio (*Demetrio*, 1731). See Livermore, "'Così fan tutte': A Well-Kept Secret" and Brown, *W. A. Mozart Così fan tutte.*

6. Brown, *W. A. Mozart Così fan tutte*, 60ff.

7. Bandera, "*Monda y desnuda,*" 246.

8. Iole Scamuzzi, "Los dos amigos: Boccaccio, Cervantes, Guillén de Castro."

9. Iole Scamuzzi, *Il "curioso impertinente" fra Spagna e Italia* (Alessandria, Italy: Edizioni dell'Orso, 2010).

10. "Il Curioso affascina il mondo delle accademie del primo Seicento, poi tace per un secolo e rifiorisce nel teatro per influenza dello spagnolo Guillén de Castro" (Scamuzzi, *Il "curioso impertinente" fra Spagna e Italia*, 205) [*author's translation*].

11. Kramer, "Da Pontes Così fan tutte."

12. See Kramer, "Da Pontes Così fan tutte," 17–18. It is interesting to emphasize here that for Link, this thematic motif plays a crucial role in *Così*, in that it triggers the appearance of "feelings of love in the previously unresponsive lovers" (Link, "*L'arbore di Diana*," 225). Without wishing to get ahead of ourselves, it is also possible that this rekindling of the women's love after the apparent suicide attempt is due to their fear of losing the object of their desire, something that makes it even more desirable.

13. Information on the recovery of this work can be found at https://shakespeareobra.wordpress.com/cardenio/.

14. Livermore, "'Così fan tutte': A Well-Kept Secret."

15. In fact, Kramer was highly critical of Livermore's ideas about the influence of *La celosa de sí misma* in the libretto for *Così*. See Kramer, "Da Pontes Così fan tutte," 7, note 1.

16. In addition to the plays, some of the Italian buffo theater traditions, such as the maid character (*soubrette*) or the arias that were critical of women, known as *tirata misogina*, should also be taken into account. See Mellace, "Nel laboratorio di Da Ponte," 299.

17. See Brown, *W. A. Mozart Così fan tutte*, 73. In *Il "curioso impertinente" fra Spagna e Italia*, Scamuzzi studied the important role played by Goldoni's comedies in disseminating the stories and themes typical of Spanish baroque theater in Italian plays and opera. In her study she focuses mainly on the relationship between *Il bugiardo* (1748) and the tradition of *El curioso impertinente*.

18. Cochran, "Da Ponte, Mozart, Byron, Casti," 125.

19. Cochran, "Da Ponte, Mozart, Byron, Casti," 136.

20. Brown, *W. A. Mozart Così fan tutte*, 70ff.

21. René Girard, "Marivaudage and Hypocrisy," *American Society of the French Legion of Honor* Magazine, 34/3 (1963), 163–174. Also in René Girard, "Marivaudage, Hypocrisy and Bad Faith." In *Mimesis and Theory. Essays on Literature and Criticism, 1953–2005* (Stanford University Press, 2008), 71–79. A Spanish translation is also available: René Girard, "Marivaudage e hipocresía," in *Geometrías del deseo* (Barcelona: Sexto Piso, 2012), 93–104.

22. Brown, *W. A. Mozart Così fan tutte*, 75ff.

23. Link, "*L'arbore di Diana*."

24. Goehring, *Three Modes*, 122–196.

25. Goehring, *Three Modes*, 124.

26. Brown, *W. A. Mozart Così fan tutte*, 60ff.

27. Hunter states that none of these works "is indisputably a source," as they "may have well constituted a frame of reference for the audience and added to the intertextual pleasures of the work." Hunter, *Culture of Opera Buffa in Mozart's Vienna*, 248–249.

28. Brown and Rice, "Salieri's 'Così fan tutte.'"

29. This is the position defended by Bandera, who also states that this idea of intertextuality "is in no way alien to Girard's critical discourse." Cesáreo Bandera, "Où nous entraîne l'intertextualité?" in *Colloque de Cerisy. Violence et vérité. Autour de René Girard* (Paris: Grasset, 1985), 468 [*author's translation*].

30. Steptoe ("The Sources of 'Così fan tutte'") identified within the libretto of *Così* two separate currents from the older sources: that of the "wager," which probably came from the *Decameron* and *Cymbeline*, and that of the departure and subsequent disguise of the husband, which came from the story of Cephalus and Procris. *El curioso impertinente*, which Da Ponte may have known firsthand, and certainly through Anfossi's opera *Il curioso indiscreto*, offered a new blend of motifs from the two currents. This theory of two separate currents, accepted by Scamuzzi ("Ovidio e Cervantes nella cultura di Da Ponte") and cited by Brown (*W. A. Mozart Così fan tutte*), is in my opinion too radical, in that it overlooks the fact that all the stories share the same theme of desire unfulfilled. There are other incongruities in this idea of two separate currents, including that the wager motif appears quite rarely in the sources and, in those where it does, it is the only motif Da Ponte borrows from them; and that the husband leaving or being called away is also present in the stories by Boccaccio and Shakespeare, as is the action of external instigators. It is also difficult to see how the two currents come together in *El curioso impertinente*, in which there is no wager.

Chapter 4. The Novelistic Truth about the Mechanisms of Desire

1. Although Girard's ideas on mimetic desire appear in practically all his books, it is perhaps in the interviews that we find the clearest, most systematic descriptions. For example, in René Girard, *Quand ces choses commenceront. Entretiens avec Michel Treguer* (Spanish edition: *Cuando empiecen a suceder estas cosas. Conversaciones con Michel Treguer* [Madrid: Encuentro, 1996]); and René Girard, *Les origines de la culture: Entretiens avec Pierpaolo Antonello et Joao Cezar de Castro Rocha* (Spanish edition: *Los orígenes de la cultura. Conversaciones con Pierpaolo Antonello y Joao Cezar de Castro Rocha* [Madrid: Trotta, 2006]).

2. Girard, *Cuando empiecen a suceder estas cosas,* 23.

3. Girard, *Theater of Envy,* 42.

4. Girard, *Los orígenes de la cultura,* 51.

5. Girard, *Mentira romántica,* 12–13.

6. René Girard, "*To Double Business Bound*." *Essays on Literature, Mimesis, and Anthropology* (Baltimore: Johns Hopkins University Press, 1978), 55.

7. Girard, *Los orígenes de la cultura,* 53.

8. Girard, *Cuando empiecen a suceder estas cosas,* 24.

9. René Girard, *La violencia y lo sagrado* (Barcelona: Anagrama, 1983), 152.

10. Girard, *Mentira romántica,* 49ff.

11. Girard, *Mentira romántica,* 91.

12. Girard, *Cuando empiecen a suceder estas cosas,* 25.

13. Girard, *Los orígenes de la cultura*, 52.

14. Girard, *Los orígenes de la cultura*, 62.

15. Girard, *Los orígenes de la cultura*, 70.

16. Spanish translations of some of these books are available: *Literatura, mímesis y antropología* (Barcelona: Gędisa, 2016), *Mentira romántica y verdad novelesca* (Madrid: Anagrama, 1985, 2nd ed. 2023), *Shakespeare. Los fuegos de la envidia* (Madrid: Anagrama, 1995, 2nd ed. 2016), and *Geometrías del deseo* (Barcelona: Sexto Piso, 2012).

17. In the meantime, the search for texts that provided mimetic revelation had led Girard to the study of mythology and the Bible, thus greatly broadening his findings, which were set out in fundamental books such as *La violence et le sacré* (1972) and *Le bouc émissaire* (1982). For a complete list of René Girard's publications, see James Alison and Wolfgang Palaver, "Girard's Works," in *The Palgrave Handbook of Mimetic Theory and Religion* (New York: Palgrave Macmillan, 2017), vii–xi.

18. Girard, "*To Double Business Bound*," 199–200.

19. Girard, "*To Double Business Bound*," vii.

20. Girard, *Mentira romántica,* 21.

21. Girard, *Cuando empiecen a suceder estas cosas,* 26, 27.

22. Girard, *Mentira romántica,* 22.

23. Girard, *Los orígenes de la cultura*, 77.

24. Girard, "*To Double Business Bound*," x.

25. "Rien d'essentiel ne sépare la littérature des autres phénomènes culturels. . . . C'est pourquoi nous pouvons dire que tout est comme la fiction littéraire et que la fiction littéraire est comme tout le reste." Bandera, "Où nous entraîne l'intertextualité?" 468 [*author's translation*].

26. Girard, "*To Double Business Bound*," x.

27. "L'adjonction du médiateur à la relation duelle sujet-objet y ajoute une deuxième dimension qui définit un *espace*—certes encore métaphorique—du desir." Eric L. Gans, "Désir, représentation, culture," in *Colloque de Cerisy. Violence et vérité. Autour de René Girard* (Paris: Grasset, 1985), 395 [*author's translation*].

28. Philippe Godefroid, "Opéra et mythe, 7. Entretien avec René Girard," *L'Avant scène opéra* 76 (juin, 1985): 115–116.

29. "On se trouve donc renvoyé à un simple jeu de doubles, où l'identité a moins d'importance que la rivalité"; "il suffit de se déguiser, ou bien de se masquer, de battre les cartes autrement, pour que les coeurs battent autrement." Girard, quoted

in Godefroid, "Opéra et mythe, 7. Entretien avec René Girard," 115 [*author's translation*].

30. "On se rend bien compte que l'effacement du discours mimétique et de la violence collective maquille et modifie complètement la vraie problématique." "Dans *L'Or* la lecture par le désir mimétique s'impose. Elle est là, à nu, explicite, dès lors que l'oeuvre est entièrement bâtie sur les mécanismes du désir et des doubles." Girard, quoted in Godefroid, "Opéra et mythe, 7. Entretien avec René Girard," 115 [*author's translation*].

31. Interestingly enough, the same review announced that Godefroid was preparing a stage production of *The Flying Dutchman* "selon l'exemple girardien" (according to the Girardian example). Philippe Godefroid, "Opéra et mythe, 7. Comment le navire hollandais devint-il le légendaire Vaisseau fantôme?" *L'Avant scène opéra* 76 (juin, 1985): 119–122, 119.

32. Girard, *Cuando empiecen a suceder estas cosas,* 26.

33. Girard, *Cuando empiecen a suceder estas cosas,* 26.

34. Girard, *Cuando empiecen a suceder estas cosas,* 26.

35. In their article on Shakespeare in opera, Wilson, Sternfeld, and White state that Shakespeare is "the single most popular source of inspiration for opera," and count as many as 270 operas based on his works, while acknowledging that only a few remain on the regular operatic repertoire, of which Giuseppe Verdi's three masterpieces *Falstaff, Otello,* and *Macbeth* are the best-known. Christopher R. Wilson, F. W. Sternfeld, and Eric Walter White, "Shakespeare, William," *Grove Music Online*, 2002; https://doi.org/10.1093/gmo/9781561592630.article.25567.

36. Philippe Godefroid, "Opéra et mythe, 7. Esquisse d'un rapprochement Wagner-Girard," *L'Avant scène opéra*, 76 (juin, 1985): 116–118; Godefroid, "Opéra et mythe, 7. Comment le navire hollandaise devint-il le légendaire Vaisseau fantôme?"

37. The article, which is not dated, can be downloaded from the official website of the Dutch Girard Society: http://girard.nl/index.php/boeken-teksten/online-teksten. It appears to be from 2009, as evidenced by the dates in the bibliography it lists, the most recent being from that year, and by the fact that the next article by this author in the list of the website is dated 2009.

38. Daniel Villegas, *Mimetologies: Aesthetic Politics in Early Modern Opera* (PhD diss., University of Pennsylvania, 2016).

39. Benoît Chantre, *Les derniers jours de René Girard* (Paris: Grasset, 2016).

40. The famous, revolutionary claim that "in opera, poetry must be the obedient daughter of music" was coined by Mozart in 1781, in one of the numerous letters he sent to his father, Leopold. Later in this same letter, Mozart lucidly affirmed that in an opera, "the music predominates absolutely and, listening to it, one forgets everything else." Wolfgang A. Mozart, *Correspondance. III. (1778–1781)* (Paris: Flammarion, 1989), 264 [*author's translation*].

41. We could also include the stage director, the conductor, and even the performers (actor-singers and musicians). Some of their contributions will also be taken into account in my analysis.

42. In the extensive bibliography about *Così fan tutte,* there are researchers, such as Farnsworth, Ford, and Goehring, who defend the need to analyze the poetry and the music together in order to be able to understand the meaning of the opera (Rodney Farnsworth, "*Così fan tutte* as Parody and Burlesque," *Opera Quarterly* 6, 2 (1988): 50–68; Ford, *Così? Sexual politics in Mozart's Operas* and *Music, Sexuality and the Enlightenment*; Goehring, *Three Modes*). For Goehring, for example, the script and the music of *Così*, far from being incompatible as some scholars have claimed, were worked on jointly "in ways unparalleled in other Mozart operas" (*Three Modes*, 28). The musical analyses offered by Ford of almost all the important musical numbers in the opera were based on his own method, which was centered on harmonic aspects that he believed enable us to understand the way the music is expressing the dramatic action and the feelings of the characters. Other authors, such as Steptoe, Brown, and Polzonetti, also included a considerable number of musical analyses that took the interaction between words and music into account, albeit without making an explicit defense of its importance. See Steptoe, "The Sources of 'Così fan tutte'"; Brown, *W. A. Mozart Così fan tutte;* and Polzonetti, "Mesmerizing Adultery."

Chapter 5. Mimetic Revelation in *Così fan tutte*

1. Girard, *Mentira romántica,* 50.
2. Girard, *Mentira romántica,* 50.
3. Girard, "*To Double Business Bound*."
4. Girard, "*To Double Business Bound*," 3.
5. Girard, *Mentira romántica,* 93.
6. Girard, *Mentira romántica,* 95.
7. Kunze, *Las óperas de Mozart*, 491.
8. Kunze, *Las óperas de Mozart*, 530.
9. In fact, the degree to which they coincide confirms my suspicions that expressions of mimetic behavior can be found in *Così fan tutte*, in this way introducing Girard into discussions about opera, a genre that has largely been ignored in mimetic theory research.
10. Heartz, "Trois écoles des amants," 19.
11. Some English translators add the word "women," ambiguously absent in the original Italian. See, for example, the translated libretto in Burton D. Fischer, *Mozart's Da Ponte Operas: The Marriage of Figaro, Don Giovanni, Cosi Fan Tutte* (Opera Journeys Publishing, 2006).
12. Brown and Rice, "Salieri's '*Così fan tutte*,'" 27.

13. I cannot find any references to this wordplay in the specialized bibliography on *Così fan tutte*, although Noiray pointed out the similarity between "nessun lo sa" and the motto "Così fan tutte," as well as the use of the phoenix metaphor cited by Metastasio. Michel Noiray, "*Così fan tutte*. Commentaire littéraire et musical," *Così fan tutte. L'Avant scène opéra* 131–132 (mai-juin, 1990): 39–141.

14. This difference was pointed out by Noiray, "Commentaire littéraire et musical," 50.

15. "Elles fondent leurs voix dans une écriture par tierces, et tiennent un discours rigoureusement identique jusqu'à la fin du morceau." (Noiray, "Commentaire littéraire et musical," 51) [*author's translation*].

16. Brown, *W. A. Mozart Così fan tutte*, 111.

17. Brown, *W. A. Mozart Così fan tutte*, 111.

18. Brown, *W. A. Mozart Così fan tutte*, 114.

19. These changes in the doubles' attitudes have been pointed out by various opera scholars, including Brèque, "Prima la musica, dopo le parole," 150.

20. Heartz, "Trois écoles des amants," 19.

21. "L'épreuve n'apparaît pas comme un jeu formel engendrant une désillusion brutale, mais comme une étape indispensable au progres du coeur et de la raison." Moindrot, "*Così fan tutte* ou les artifices de l'idéal," 32 [*author's translation*].

22. Hunter, *Così fan tutte et les conventions musicaux de son temps* and *Culture of Opera Buffa in Mozart's Vienna*.

23. Girard, *Theater of Envy*, 123.

24. René Girard, El misterio de nuestro mundo. Claves para una interpretación antropológica. Diálogos con *J. M. Oughourlian y G. Lefort* (Salamanca, Spain: Ediciones Sígueme, 1982), 380–381.

25. Kunze, *Las óperas de Mozart*, 476.

26. Steptoe, *Mozart-Da Ponte Operas,* 235.

27. Girard, "*To Double Business Bound*."

28. Girard, "*To Double Business Bound*," 2.

29. In Italian, "indiscreto" is used to refer to people who talk deceitfully at great length and with no substance.

30. Girard, "Marivaudage, Hypocrisy and Bad Faith," 71.

31. Girard, "Marivaudage, Hypocrisy and Bad Faith," 73.

32. For example, for Polzonetti this number is like a hypnosis session in which the intention is to control the desires of the two women. He provides quite a convincing analysis of the music in support of this claim (Polzonetti, "Mesmerizing Adultery," 284–287).

33. Girard, "Marivaudage, Hypocrisy and Bad Faith," 72.

34. Vignal, "Sources, composition et créateurs."

35. Moindrot, "*Così fan tutte* ou les artifices de l'idéal."

36. "C'est lors de cette scène que les personnages se touchent pour la première fois. La contagion physique, en outre, est clairement transposée dans le finale par la contagion musicale grâce à laquelle les individus peuvent libremente exprimer leurs pensées contradictoires, et dans le concert général perdre un instant leur singularité." Moindrot, "*Così fan tutte* ou les artifices de l'idéal," 29 [*author's translation*].

37. Polzonetti, "Mesmerizing Adultery."

38. Girard, *Theater of Envy*.

39. Kunze, *Las óperas de Mozart*, 514.

40. Brown, *W. A. Mozart Così fan tutte*, 144.

41. Patricia Lewy, "Mozart's Fiordiligi: Adriana Ferrarese del Bene," *Cambridge Opera Journal*, 8, 3 (1996): 199–214, 213.

42. "L'air de Fiordiligi . . . presente la caractéristique de s'ouvrir sur un Adagio, qui révèle une introspection particullièrement profonde et douloureuse" (Noiray, "Commentaire littéraire et musical," 113) [*author's translation*].

43. "L'emploi des cors, qui semblent representer, dans la tradition française . . . la voix de l'être aimé absent," "les cors sont aussi pour Mozart la métaphore des 'cornes' du cocu" (Noiray, "Commentaire littéraire et musical," 113) [*author's translation*].

44. Brown, *W. A. Mozart Così fan tutte*, 132ff.

45. Goehring, *Three Modes*, 238.

46. Mellace, "Nel laboratorio di Da Ponte," 284.

47. Almost all *Così* scholars have analyzed the duet between Fiordiligi and Ferrando, "Fra gli amplessi," in depth, given that it represents a crucial moment in the opera, the fall of Fiordiligi. Some highlights include perceptive remarks by Ford in *Così? Sexual Politics in Mozart's Operas*, 187–209, and in *Music, Sexuality and the Enlightenment*, 161–171; Polzonetti in "Mesmerizing Adultery," 287–290; and Goehring in *Three Modes*, 246–259.

48. "L'intervention de Ferrando, juste après la cadence en *mi*, est d'une extraordinaire efficacité, dans la mesure où elle combine les caractères contradictoires d'une continuation et d'une interruption." Noiray, "Commentaire littéraire et musical," 125 [*author's translation*].

49. Hunter, "Some Representations of Opera Seria," 106. See also Hunter, *Culture of Opera Buffa in Mozart's Vienna*.

50. Steptoe, *Mozart-Da Ponte Operas*, 242.

51. Kunze, *Las óperas de Mozart*, 156.

52. "Avec Ferrando, Mozart trahit en fait le sens du livret" (Brèque, "Prima la musica,

dopo le parole," 156) [*author's translation*].

53. "Ah, no, no, you shall not depart! / No, cruel, you will not go! / I'd sooner tear out my heart! / I'd rather die at your feet!"

54. Steptoe, *Mozart-Da Ponte Operas,* 216.

55. Steptoe, *Mozart-Da Ponte Operas,* 229.

56. See Brown, *W. A. Mozart Così fan tutte,* 127–128, for a detailed analysis of the orchestration of this number.

57. Hunter, "Some Representations of Opera Seria," 94, 99.

58. Hunter, "Some Representations of Opera Seria," 99.

59. Kramer, "Da Pontes Così fan tutte"; Farnsworth, "*Così fan tutte* as Parody and Burlesque"; Rosen, *El estilo clásico*; Kunze, *Las óperas de Mozart*; Steptoe, *Mozart-Da Ponte Operas;* Brown, *W. A. Mozart Così fan tutte*; Lewy, "Mozart's Fiordiligi"; and Goehring, *Three Modes*.

60. Rosen, *El estilo clásico*, 362.

61. Lewy, "Mozart's Fiordiligi."

62. Brown, *W. A. Mozart Così fan tutte,* 128ff. This parodic vision of "Come scoglio" had already been put forward by Kramer ("Da Pontes Così fan tutte") and Farnsworth ("*Così fan tutte* as Parody and Burlesque"). The latter's analysis emphasizes the importance of the parody of the tragic style in *Così*, which is evident not just in this particular number but throughout the entire work. He claims that it should not be seen simply as the insertion of a comic ingredient into the text, but more as the means by which the opera defends rational thought against the "heroic-chivalric world."

63. Hunter, "Some Representations of Opera Seria."

64. Hunter, "Some Representations of Opera Seria," 107.

65. Steptoe, *Mozart-Da Ponte Operas,* 216, 223.

66. Steptoe, *Mozart-Da Ponte Operas,* 225.

67. Kunze, *Las óperas de Mozart,* 486.

68. Kunze, *Las óperas de Mozart,* 492.

69. Steptoe, *Mozart-Da Ponte Operas,* 229.

70. Girard, "Marivaudage, Hypocrisy and Bad Faith," 74, 76.

71. Girard, "Marivaudage, Hypocrisy and Bad Faith," 72.

72. Ford, *Così? Sexual Politics in Mozart's Operas* and *Music, Sexuality and the Enlightenment*; Natošević, "*Così fan tutte*"*: Mozart, die Liebe und die Revolution von 1789*; Cochran, "Da Ponte, Mozart, Byron, Casti"; and Giuseppe Gazzola, "Betting Against Themselves: Conflicting Conceptions of Love in *Così fan tutte, o: la scola degli amanti*," *Modern Language Notes* 130, 1 (2015): 105–123.

73. "La résolution du drame se fait par la reconnaissance de l'illusion qui, au-delà du fleuve mouvant des apparences, permet d'envisager une image sereine de l'éternel." Moindrot, "*Così fan tutte* ou les artifices de l'idéal," 34 [*author's translation*].

74. "Gombrich mag hier mit Recht vermuten, daß Da Ponte einem auf Humanität begründeten vernünftigen Verhalten das Wort reden wollte. . . . Das rationale Verzeihen als Prinzip zur Lösung des tragischen Konfliktes." Kramer, "Da Pontes Così fan tutte," 25–26 [*author's translation*].

75. Hunter, *Culture of Opera Buffa in Mozart's Vienna*, 296.

76. Farnsworth, "*Così fan tutte* as Parody and Burlesque," 64.

77. Goehring, *Three Modes*, 217.

78. See in particular the chapter "The Philosophical Mode" (53–121), which is devoted to the study of this character and includes a musical analysis of his singing style, which Goehring believes is original and unprecedented in opera and which he defines as "the musical equivalent of the aphorism" (Goehring, *Three Modes*, 95).

79. Lucien Goldmann, *Pour un sociologie du roman* (Paris: Gallimard, 1964), 22, quoted in Girard, "*To Double Business Bound*," 5.

80. "Quanto disio / menò costoro al doloroso passo!" [Longfellow's translation, retrieved from https://digitaldante.columbia.edu/].

81. Girard, *Theater of Envy*, 48.

82. Girard, "*To Double Business Bound*," 5.

83. "Les valeurs auxquelles on croyait ont été relativisées ou subverties" (Brèque, "Prima la musica, dopo le parole," 152) [*author's translation*].

84. Bandera, "*Monda y desnuda*."

85. Girard, *Theater of Envy*, chapter 37.

86. Kunze, *Las óperas de Mozart*, 478.

87. Kunze, *Las óperas de Mozart*, 481, 486.

88. Kunze, *Las óperas de Mozart*, 486.

Epilogue. Revealing the Truth of Human Emotions

1. Rosen, *El estilo clásico*; Farnsworth, "*Così fan tutte* as Parody and Burlesque"; Steptoe, *Mozart-Da Ponte Operas;* Brèque, "Prima la musica, dopo le parole"; Moindrot, "*Così fan tutte* ou les artifices de l'idéal"; Hunter, "Some Representations of Opera Seria" and *Culture of Opera Buffa in Mozart's Vienna*; and Goehring, *Three Modes*.

2. Kunze, *Las óperas de Mozart*, 471.

3. Kunze, *Las óperas de Mozart*, 484.

4. Kunze, *Las óperas de Mozart*, 477.

5. René Girard, "Perilous Balance: A Comic Hypothesis," later included in Girard, "*To Double Business Bound*."

6. Girard, "*To Double Business Bound*," 125.

7. Goehring offers, in *Three Modes of Perception in Mozart*, a convincing explanation as to the meaning of the opera as a comedy. In his conclusions he states that if *Così* allows us to understand more about human nature, it is precisely because it presents it from its comic side. In his opinion, comedy in this opera is perceived "not as an assertion of superiority but as an instrument of acceptance and reconciliation." (Goehring, *Three Modes*, 270).

8. Girard, "*To Double Business Bound*," 127.

Bibliography

Classical Sources of the Libretto Cited in the Book (Spanish Editions)

Ariosto, Ludovico. *Orlando furioso*. Barcelona: Espasa Libros, 2017.

Boccaccio, Giovanni. *De las mujeres ilustres (De mulieribus claris)*. Cuban Artists Around the World, 2021.

Boccaccio, Giovanni. *Decameron*. Barcelona: Espasa-Calpe, Austral Narrativa, 2007.

Cervantes, Miguel de. *Don Quijote de la Mancha, I y II*. Madrid: Cátedra, Letras Hispánicas, 2005.

Hyginus. *Fábulas*. Madrid: Biblioteca Clásica Gredos, 2009.

Livy, Titus. *Historia de Roma desde su fundación. Libros I-III.* Madrid: Biblioteca Clásica Gredos, 2016.

Ovid. *Fastos*. Madrid: Biblioteca Clásica Gredos, 1988.

Ovid. *Metamorfosis VI-X*. Madrid: Biblioteca Clásica Gredos, 2016.

Pseudo-Apollodorus. *Biblioteca mitológica*. Madrid: Editorial Gredos, 1985.

Shakespeare, William. *Cimbelino*. Madrid: Editorial Gredos, 2003.

Other Works Cited

Alison, James, and Wolfgang Palaver. (2017). "Girard's Works." In *The Palgrave Handbook of Mimetic Theory and Religion*, vii–xi. New York: Palgrave Macmillan, 2017.

Bandera, Cesáreo. "*Monda y desnuda*:" *la humilde historia de Don Quijote*. Biblioteca Aurea Hispánica, 37. Madrid: Editorial Iberoamericana, 2005.

Bandera, Cesáreo. "Où nous entraîne l'intertextualité?" In *Colloque de Cerisy. Violence et vérité. Autour de René Girard*, edited by Paul Dumouchel, 468–482. Paris: Grasset, 1985.

Brèque, Jean-Michel. "Prima la musica, dopo le parole." *Così fan tutte. L'Avant scène opéra* 131–132 (mai-juin, 1990): 146–157.

Brown, Bruce Alan. *W. A. Mozart Così fan tutte*. Cambridge Opera Handbooks. Cambridge: Cambridge University Press, 1995.

Brown, Bruce Alan, and John A. Rice. "Salieri's 'Così fan tutte,'" *Cambridge Opera Journal* 8, 1 (March 1996): 17–43.

Caruso, Carlo. "'Così fan tutte,' o sia la scuola dell' 'Orlando furioso.'" *Il Saggiatore musicale* 1, 2 (1994): 361–375.

Chantre, Benoît. *Les derniers jours de René Girard*. Paris: Grasset, 2016.

Cochran, Peter. "Da Ponte, Mozart, Byron, Casti: A Question of Dimensions." In *Byron and Women (and Men)*, 125–145. Newcastle: Cambridge Scholars, 2010.

Dent, Edward J. *Mozart's Operas: A Critical Study* (2nd edition, London: Oxford University Press, 1947).

Edge, Dexter. "Mozart's Fee for *Così fan tutte*." *Journal of the Royal Musical Association* 116 (1991): 211–235.

Einstein, Alfred. *Mozart: His Character, His Work* (New York: Oxford University Press, 1945).

Farnsworth, Rodney. "*Così fan tutte* as Parody and Burlesque." *Opera Quarterly* 6, 2 (1988): 50–68.

Fischer, Burton D. *Mozart's Da Ponte Operas: The Marriage of Figaro, Don Giovanni, Cosi Fan Tutte* (Opera Journeys Publishing, 2006).

Ford, Charles. *Così? Sexual Politics in Mozart's Operas*. Manchester: Manchester University Press, 1991.

Ford, Charles. *Music, Sexuality and the Enlightenment in Mozart's Figaro, Don Giovanni and Così fan tutte*. Farnham, U.K.: Ashgate, 2012.

Gans, Eric L. "Désir, représentation, culture." In *Colloque de Cerisy. Violence et vérité. Autour de René Girard*, edited by Paul Dumouchel, 395–404. Paris: Grasset, 1985.

Gazzola, Giuseppe. "Betting Against Themselves: Conflicting Conceptions of Love in *Così fan tutte, o: la scola degli amanti*." *Modern Language Notes* 130, 1 (2015): 105–123.

Girard, René. "El deseo mimético (Shakespeare mejor que Platón)." In *Cuando empiecen a suceder estas cosas. Conversaciones con Michel Treguer*, translated by Ángel Barahona, 23–30. Madrid: Encuentro, 1996. (Original edition: *Quand ces choses commenceront. Entretiens avec Michel Treguer*, 1994.)

Girard, René. *La violencia y lo sagrado*. Translated by Joaquín Jordá. Barcelona: Anagrama, 1983. (Original edition: *La violence et le sacré*, 1972.)

Girard, René. "Latencia y rivalidad mimética." In *El misterio de nuestro mundo. Claves para una interpretación antropológica. Diálogos con J. M. Oughourlian y G. Lefort*, translated by Alfonso Ortiz, 376–385. Salamanca, Spain: Ediciones Sígueme, 1982. (Original edition: *Des choses cachées depuis la fondation du monde. Recherches avec J. M. Oughourlian et G. Lefort*, 1978.)

Girard, René. "Marivaudage, Hypocrisy and Bad Faith." In *Mimesis and Theory: Essays on Literature and Criticism, 1953–2005* (Stanford, CA: Stanford University Press, 2008), 71–79. (Original edition: "Marivaudage and Hypocrisy," 1963.)

Girard, René. *Mentira romántica y verdad novelesca*. Translated by Joaquín Jordá. Barcelona: Anagrama, 1985, 2nd ed. 2023. (Original edition: *Mensonge romantique et vérité romanesque*, 1961.)

Girard, René. *A Theater of Envy: William Shakespeare* (Oxford: Oxford University Press, 1991).

Girard, René. "*To Double Business Bound*": *Essays on Literature, Mimesis, and Anthropology* (Baltimore: Johns Hopkins University Press, 1978).

Girard, René. "'Una teoría con la que se puede trabajar': el mecanismo mimético." In *Los orígenes de la cultura. Conversaciones con Pierpaolo Antonello y Joao Cezar de Castro Rocha*, translated by José Luis San Miguel, 51–81. Madrid: Trotta, 2006. (Original edition: *Les origines de la culture*, 2004.)

Godefroid, Philippe. "Opéra et mythe, 7. Comment le navire hollandais devint-il le légendaire Vaisseau fantôme?" *L'Avant scène opéra 76* (juin, 1985): 119–122.

Godefroid, Philippe. "Opéra et mythe, 7. Entretien avec René Girard." *L'Avant scène opéra* 76 (juin, 1985): 115–116.

Godefroid, Philippe. "Opéra et mythe, 7. Esquisse d'un rapprochement Wagner-Girard." *L'Avant scène opéra* 76 (juin, 1985): 116–118.

Goehring, Edmund J. *Three Modes of Perception in Mozart: The Philosophical, Pastoral, and Comic in* Così fan tutte. Cambridge: Cambridge University Press, 2004.

Gombrich, Ernst H. "Cosi fan tutte (Procris Included)." *Journal of the Warburg Courtauld Institutes* xvii (1954): 372–374.

Heartz, Daniel. "Mozart and Da Ponte." *The Musical Quarterly* 79, 4 (Winter, 1995): 700–718.

Heartz, Daniel. *Mozart's Operas*. Berkeley: University of California Press, 1990.

Heartz, Daniel. "Trois écoles des amants. *Così fan tutte*." *L'Avant scène opéra* 131–132 (mai-juin, 1990): 16–22.

Hunter, Mary. "*Così fan tutte* et les conventions musicaux de son temps." *Così fan tutte. L'Avant scène opéra* 131–132 (mai-juin,1990): 158–164.

Hunter, Mary. *The Culture of Opera Buffa in Mozart's Vienna: A Poetics of Entertainment.* Princeton, N.J.: Princeton University Press, 1999.

Hunter, Mary. "Some Representations of Opera Seria in Opera Buffa." *Cambridge Opera Journal* 3, 2 (July 1991): 89–108.

Keefe, Simon P. *Mozart in Vienna: The Final Decade.* Cambridge: Cambridge University Press, 2017.

Kramer, Kurt. "Da Pontes Così fan tutte." *Nachrichten der Akademie der Wissenschaften in Göttingen, 1. Philologisch-historische Klasse* 1 (1973): 3–27.

Kunze, Stefan. "Così fan tutte. Bromas serias." In *Las óperas de Mozart,* translated by Ambrosio Berasain, 469–562. Madrid: Alianza Editorial, 1990. (Original edition: *Mozarts Opern,* 1984.)

Lewy, Patricia. "Mozart's Fiordiligi: Adriana Ferrarese del Bene." *Cambridge Opera Journal* 8, 3 (1996): 199–214.

Link, Dorothea. "*L'arbore di Diana*: A Model for *Così fan tutte*." In *Wolfgang Amadè Mozart: Essays on his Life and his Music,* edited by Stanley Sadie, 362–376. New York: Oxford University Press-Clarendon Press, 1996.

Livermore, Ann. "'Così fan tutte': A Well-Kept Secret." *Music & Letters* 46, 4 (1965): 316–321.

Mellace, Raffaele. "Nel laboratorio di Da Ponte: *Così fan tutte, Le nozze di Figaro* e la librettistica coeva." *Rivista Italiana di Musicologia* 33, 2 (1998): 279–300.

Moindrot, Isabelle. "*Così fan tutte* ou les artifices de l'idéal." *Così fan tutte. L'Avant scène opéra* 131–132 (mai-juin, 1990): 23–34.

Mozart, Wolfgang A. *Correspondance. III. (1778–1781).* Paris: Flammarion, 1989.

Natošević, Constanze. "*Così fan tutte*": *Mozart, die Liebe und die Revolution von 1789.* Kassel, Germany: Bärenreiter, 2003.

Noiray, Michel. "*Così fan tutte.* Commentaire littéraire et musical." *Così fan tutte. L'Avant scène opéra* 131–132 (mai-juin, 1990): 39–141.

Polzonetti, Pierpaolo. "Mesmerizing Adultery: *Così fan tutte* and the Kornman Scandal." *Cambridge Opera Journal* 14, 3 (2002): 263–296.

Robins, Brian. "*Così* and Ariosto." *Musical Times* 123, 1676 (October 1982): 666.

Rosen, Charles. "La ópera cómica." In *El estilo clásico: Haydn, Mozart, Beethoven,* 333–374. translated by Elena Giménez. Madrid: Alianza Editorial, 1999. (Original edition: *The Classical Style: Haydn, Mozart, Beethoven,* 1971.)

Scamuzzi, Iole. "*El curioso impertinente* de Cervantes: tragedia barroca y ópera buffa." In *Recreaciones teatrales y alegorías cervantinas,* edited by Carlos Mata, 135–141. Navarra, Spain: EUNSA-Publicaciones de literatura-Departamento de Filología, 2012.

Scamuzzi. Iole. *Il "curioso impertinente" fra Spagna e Italia.* Alessandria, Italy: Edizioni dell'Orso, 2010.

Scamuzzi, Iole. "Los dos amigos: Boccaccio, Cervantes, Guillén de Castro." In *Rumbos del hispanismo en el umbral del Cincuentenario de la Asociación Internacional de Hispanistas.* (Proceedings of the Seventeenth AIH Congress), edited by Patrizia Botta, Aviva Garribba, María Luisa Cerrón, and Debora Vaccari, 217–222. Roma: Bagatto Libri, 2012.

Scamuzzi, Iole. "Ovidio e Cervantes nella cultura di Da Ponte: alle radici del 'Così fan tutte.'" *Lettere Italiane* 56, 3 (2004): 468–483.

Scamuzzi, Iole. "Tra Bradamante e Fiordiligi c'è Camila: la novella del *Curioso Impertinente* come fonte del libretto di *Così Fan Tutte.*" *Artifara* 4 (2004): 211–221.

Steptoe, Andrew. *Mozart-Da Ponte Operas: The Cultural and Musical Background to Le Nozze Di Figaro, Don Giovanni, and Cosi Fan Tutte.* Oxford: Clarendon Paperbacks, 1990.

Steptoe, Andrew. "The Sources of 'Così fan tutte': A Reappraisal." *Music & Letters* 62, 3/4 (1981): 281–294.

Téllez, José Luis. "¿Sólo un cuento (in)moral?" In *Così fan tutte. Teatro Real. Temporada 2001–2002.* Madrid: Fundación del Teatro Lírico, 2001.

Vignal, Marc. "Sources, composition et créateurs." *Così fan tutte. L'Avant scène opéra* 131–132 (mai-juin 1990): 6–15.

Villegas, Daniel. *Mimetologies: Aesthetic Politics in Early Modern Opera.* PhD diss., University of Pennsylvania, 2016.

Vorstenbosch, Berry. "Against the Grain: Mimetic Theory and the Case of Boris Godunov." Girard studiekring-Dutch Girard Society, n.d. [2009?]. Retrieved from https://www.girard.nl/texts_online/v/Vorstenbosch_Berry_2.pdf.

Wilson, Christopher R., F. W. Sternfeld, and Eric Walter White. "Shakespeare, William." *Grove Music Online.* 2002; https://doi.org/10.1093/gmo/9781561592630.article.25567.

Wolff, Christoph. *Mozart en el umbral de su plenitud. Al servicio del emperador (1788–1791).* Translated by Ramón Andrés. Barcelona: Acantilado, 2018. (Original edition: *Mozart at the Gateway to His Fortune. Serving the Emperor (1788–1791)*, 2012.)

Index

R

S

V

W